The Brookings Institution: A Fifty-Year History

The Brookings Institution

A FIFTY-YEAR HISTORY

by
Charles B. Saunders, Jr.

Published by the Institution
WASHINGTON, D.C.
1966

Contents

Foreword

THE BROOKINGS INSTITUTION has played a special role in research and education on public problems, and exercised substantial influence on the formulation of national policy. This brief narrative of its origins, its development, and its accomplishments is appropriately issued during the fiftieth anniversary of its founding.

The book provides the first full account of how the present institution came into being. A history of the *Institute for Government Research*, the first of three antecedent organizations, was prepared by Charles A. H. Thomson and published in 1956. A *Directory of Staff and Publications 1916–1961* was issued in 1963.

The author, Charles B. Saunders, Jr., is Assistant to the President. He has been writing about Brookings activities since 1961, when he placed the Institution on an annual reporting basis. His account of *The Advanced Study Program*, the Brookings conferences for leaders in public and private life, was issued in 1962.

ROBERT D. CALKINS
President

August 1, 1966

I

THE PRESENT

Knowledge in the Service of Mankind

Brookings has earned the esteem of public officials of all com-plexions. And though it is private and nongovernmental, it is an institution of the American people. Its recognition stems from the insights Brookings research has provided into a variety of major policy issues—from the quality of these insights and from their usefulness. . . . The Brookings ideal epitomizes knowledge in the service of mankind.

HENRY HEALD, NOVEMBER 17, 1960

APPROPRIATELY ENOUGH for an institution which has survived and thrived in Washington for fifty years, Brookings is many things to many people. To decision-makers in public and private life and specialists in and out of government, Brookings is a source of independent analysis of economic, social, and political problems confronting the United States. To several thousand federal executives, it is a nonpartisan private agency which helps develop their capacities for broader career responsibilities. To hundreds of business executives and labor leaders, Brookings has brought fuller awareness and appreciation of the problems of government and the intricacies of national policy issues.

In the academic community, Brookings is known for its contributions to economic and governmental research. It also serves as a center for advanced study for scholars from all over the world, and provides research training for a select group of younger men and women.

In some of the nation's major metropolitan areas, Brookings is helping local officials and civic leaders achieve a better grasp of the urban problems affecting their communities.

To some, Brookings is a Washington landmark; to others it is a seminar in Colonial Williamsburg. Many college students know it mainly as a publisher of required reading. Some liberals consider the Institution a bit too conservative; some conservatives suspect it is a shade too liberal. Most Americans who have heard of Brookings know it only vaguely as a "respected research organization."

These are among the images of an institution which for half a century has been contributing to the strength and vitality of American society. But their sum hardly conveys the substance of what Brookings is today.

In conception and structure, Brookings is unique. Other institutions share some of its research interests or perform some similar educational services, but no other private organization combines its broad range of policy interests with its fundamental commitment to make social science research useful to leaders throughout society. No other institution of its scope or standing is present on the Washington scene conducting a critical examination of public institutions and policies in a spirit of nonpartisan public service and maintaining close relations with the government, the academic community, and the world of affairs. In the words of President Robert D. Calkins, Brookings stands as "a plot of nonpolitical territory where scholars, responsible officials in public life, and leaders in private life may meet for consideration of problems in the national interest."

Yet Brookings is not large by the standards of some other research or educational institutions. Its resident professional staff numbers about 85, with an equal number of scholars associated in a nonresident capacity. Its endowment provides about 27 percent of its $4.7 million operating budget for 1966–67. Some 34 percent of program costs are met by grants from philanthropic foundations. Government grants, contracts, and fees account for another 14 percent; individual and corporate contributions account for nearly 10 percent, and the balance is made up from sale of publications, fees, and miscellaneous other income.

Unlike many institutions, Brookings does not perform contract research for private clients or classified work for government. On request, it may undertake contract studies for government, but only on condition that its findings may be made public. Its program is shaped in a continuing dialogue between the staff and government officials, members of the academic community, and others in private life. This dialogue defines the most urgent current research needs and identifies emerging problems that suggest new challenges for research scholars and, ultimately, for decision-makers.

Over 100 projects are currently in progress in the Institution's three research divisions. Economic Studies is the largest, accounting for over a quarter of the Institution's total budget. Its investigations seek principles and methods to sustain economic growth and stability; strengthen the equity and efficiency of the tax structure; improve analysis of international payments problems; measure the impact of market structure and regulatory policy; explore the potentialities and limitations of monetary and fiscal policy; and examine the role of human resources in the growth process. Its econometric model of the U. S. economy is providing new insights into the dynamic properties of the economy and better tools for short-range forecasting. Its programs of research on issues of public finance and the role of transportation in the emerging nations are involving scholars throughout the country in the most exhaustive integrated scholarly investigations ever undertaken in these areas.

The Governmental Studies division is examining national political institutions and governing processes. Members of the Senate and House are directly involved in the work on congressional organization and policy-making, participating in off-the-record seminars. Studies of the Executive branch deal with leadership and management problems of the career service. A major program of studies of the administration of justice has recently been inaugurated.

The Foreign Policy Studies division is investigating the economic, social, and political problems of the emerging countries. Latin America is the primary focus of its attention, and its research is involving a growing number of Latin American scholars and institutions in joint efforts to compile basic data for planning economic integration of the region. Another series of studies is providing critical analysis of foreign assistance. The division is also conducting a program of research on policy problems involving the United Nations and the specialized international agencies.

Through a newly established Computer Center, the advanced concepts and techniques of electronic data processing are being applied to the Institution's research in each of the three divisions.

Brookings is a major international publisher, issuing

some twenty-five books a year and numerous other publications. Each book is presented as a competent work of responsible scholarship that is worthy of public consideration. This judgment is made by a reading committee of scholars, appointed for each project to review the manuscript. The committee's task is to judge the professional quality of the study: the author's findings and recommendations are his alone. The Institution itself does not take positions on public issues. The Publications Division edits the studies and disseminates their findings by the sale of books, issuance of brief reports summarizing their findings, distribution of some studies through commercial paperback publishers, and reprinting of professional articles written by staff members.

The Advanced Study Program plays a key role in the Institution's program, serving as an important channel for the communication of research knowledge to leaders in public and private life. Its conferences provide opportunities for officials of business, labor, and the professions, senior civil servants, members of Congress and government officials at state and local levels to improve their understanding of national and international problems. These activities serve as forums for discussion of relevant findings with the research staff and other leading specialists.

Brookings fosters policy research in the broader academic community through its Research Fellowship and Guest Scholar programs. Fellowships are awarded annually to bring younger economists and political scientists to Brookings for predoctoral or postdoctoral research. Guest Scholar appointments for varying periods make the library and study facilities available to scholars from other institutions in this country and abroad.

Fellowships are also extended to senior career officials who take leave from the federal government to work on problems of interest to their agencies, and to business executives who participate in a series of public policy seminars at Brookings while on short-term working assignments in government agencies. The conference and dining facilities of the Institution are regularly used by other nonprofit research and educational institutions and by government agencies.

As an institution of the American people, Brookings today embodies its founders' dreams more fully than ever before. Its staff is stronger, its resources larger, its plans bolder; its findings have never been more relevant and influential. The significance of its work and its achievements over the past fifty years, recounted on the following pages, provide a solid foundation for future service as the Institution enters its second half-century.

II

EARLY YEARS

The Vision of the Founders

With the increasing complexity of modern life, the scope of governmental activities will steadily and inevitably extend. No question before the people of the United States is of more urgent practical importance than this: How can the citizens exercise intelligent and effective control over their joint public business?

INSTITUTE FOR GOVERNMENT RESEARCH PROSPECTUS
MARCH 13, 1916

AMERICA'S MOOD was expansive and optimistic in early March of 1916, although the war in Europe was causing increasing concern. Germany was attacking in strength at Verdun, and French casualties in the battle already numbered 40,000, but the public was more concerned with the seventeen American lives lost in Pancho Villa's March 9 raid on Columbus, New Mexico. They applauded President Wilson's prompt dispatch of 5,000 soldiers across the border. The *New York Times* explained to the rest of the world that the action was taken "only because the Carranza government is obviously unable to preserve order," and should not be construed as armed intervention because "the Administration in Washington entertains the friendliest feelings for Mexico and desires only to help that country to establish a just and permanent government."

Business was booming. Organized medicine came out in favor of the health insurance bills then being introduced in a number of state legislatures. Organized labor denounced the doctors and opposed any "effort to force a system of compulsory health insurance upon the wage earners of the country." A snowball fight at Columbia erupted into a student riot, and at Barnard sleeveless gowns were barred from campus as too provocative.

Sports and politics were prime topics of conversation. Over a thousand people a day paid to watch Jess Willard training to defend his heavyweight title, and political journalists speculated on whom the Republicans would nominate that summer to oppose Wilson. (It was widely believed that Teddy Roosevelt would again be a candidate, on the basis of his declaration that "I will not permit any factional fight to be made in my behalf. Indeed, I will go further and say that it would be a mistake to nominate me unless the country has in its mind something of the heroic. . . . ")

An announcement issued by a group of businessmen and educators on March 13, 1916, reflected the national confidence and faith in progress. Efficiency in government organization and administration could be achieved, they declared, with two essentials:

(1) Knowledge of the best methods of administrative organization to be obtained by means of thorough scientific study, so that it may be possible to conduct governmental activities with maximum effectiveness and minimum waste.

(2) The development of active public interest in administrative efficiency.

A nonpartisan private research agency could provide these essentials, they said, by developing standards for measuring the administrative efficiency of the government. Thus they announced the founding of the Institute for Government Research in Washington.

The concept of an institute devoted to efficiency and economy appears narrow by contrast with the broad concern for public problems maintained today by the

IGR's direct descendant, the Brookings Institution. In the context of the times, however, the distinguished citizens who brought the Institute into being were far-sighted, if not visionary.

Public administration was just beginning to attract scholars. Lacking a well-defined science of administration, the IGR founders saw that the work must start by gathering rudimentary facts. Before productive analysis could be expected, surveys would have to be made "of the work of the separate government departments by themselves, [and] of the different departments and bureaus in their relation to each other, the over-lapping of functions, the duplication of effort, the lack of coordination, which is the admitted result of the manner in which departmental and governmental functions have often been expanded without systematic plan or correlation."

Government agencies had never attempted to compile such elementary organizational data, although a number of private bureaus of municipal research and citizens' commissions had begun to collect facts about state and local government. The New York Bureau of Municipal Research in particular had been notably successful in paving the way for local reforms. Its director, Frederick A. Cleveland, became convinced that a similar organization in Washington could play a useful role at the national level.

No one knew better than Cleveland how seriously federal reforms were needed. In 1911 and 1912 he had served as chairman of President Taft's Commission on

Economy and Efficiency, which made comprehensive recommendations for streamlining government organization and procedures.

The findings of the Taft Commission were ignored by Congress, but not by the influential men in business and finance, education, and philanthropy who were Cleveland's associates. He convinced them that, if the government would not attend to its own rationalization, the best hope lay in a private organization dedicated to that end. In late 1914, they held a meeting to plan how such an institution should be established.

Among the chief proponents of the concept were Charles D. Norton, Vice President of the National Bank of New York who, as assistant to President Taft, had been responsible for organizing the Commission; Jerome D. Greene, Secretary of the newly formed Rockefeller Foundation; Raymond B. Fosdick, then a New York lawyer and adviser to John D. Rockefeller Jr. in his philanthropies; churchman and educator Anson Phelps Stokes; James F. Curtis, Fosdick's law partner who had served as Assistant Secretary of the Treasury; financier R. Fulton Cutting, chairman of the New York Bureau of Municipal Research; railroad executive Charles P. Neill, a former U. S. Commissioner of Labor; banker Frederick Strauss; and Theodore N. Vail, President of the American Telephone and Telegraph Company. These nine were appointed as a steering committee to draft the organizational structure, search for a board of trustees, and arrange initial financing.

They also persuaded the Rockefeller Foundation to create a Special Committee on Scientific Research in

Governmental Problems, with funds to develop an agenda for research and provide initial support for basic studies of the kind envisioned for the Institute. Greene, Fosdick, Neill, and Norton served on this committee with William F. Willoughby, a professor of jurisprudence and politics at Princeton University who had also been a member of the Taft Commission. They authorized studies to begin under the direction of Cleveland and his staff at the Bureau of Municipal Research.

The steering committee selected prospective trustees who could provide broad national support for the Institute. Remarkably, Greene remembered, "every man we asked . . . accepted with the sole exception of a Texas ex-Congressman" whom Colonel E. M. House had suggested to him as an appropriate representative of the Southwest. Stokes suggested the name of Robert S. Brookings, President of the Corporation of Washington University. Greene traveled to St. Louis to enlist Brookings, assuring him that the chief function of the trustees would be "to vouch before the public for the integrity of the enterprise and its freedom from the slightest political bias," and that he would have no responsibility for raising funds. Brookings readily assented.

By late 1915, the list of trustees was complete. It was, Curtis later recalled, "the most distinguished group that I have ever seen in this country." In addition to Brookings, Curtis, Cutting, Fosdick, Neill, Strauss, and Vail, the original board included Edwin A. Alderman, President of the University of Virginia; Cleveland H. Dodge, Vice President of Phelps Dodge Corporation;

15

Charles W. Eliot, President Emeritus of Harvard; Felix Frankfurter, professor of law at Harvard; Frank J. Goodnow, President of Johns Hopkins University and a former member of the Taft Commission; Arthur T. Hadley, President of Yale; Mrs. E. H. Harriman of New York; James J. Hill, St. Paul railroad executive; Cesar Lombardi, Dallas publisher; A. Lawrence Lowell, President of Harvard; Samuel Mather, a Cleveland lawyer; Martin A. Ryerson, President of the Board of Trustees of the University of Chicago; Charles R. Van Hise, President of the University of Wisconsin; and Robert S. Woodward, President of the Carnegie Institution of Washington.

Forty-three donors pledged $160,000 over a five-year period, providing $30,000 a year to begin operations. The Institute was chartered March 10, 1916, and announced to the public three days later. At the organization meeting March 25, President Goodnow of Hopkins was elected Chairman of the Board and Mr. Brookings Vice Chairman. A year later Jerome Greene and Charles Norton of the original steering committee joined the board. One of the nine founders, Anson Phelps Stokes, did not accept a trusteeship until 1935.

Public reaction to the new organization was mixed. The *New Republic* of March 18 commented that "the Institute will have a unique opportunity of bringing home to Congress and to the public the price which the country is paying for its indifference and hostility to administrative honesty and efficiency. Its critical analysis of the operations of the Washington Government, accompanied by specific suggestions for methodical improvement, will strengthen the hands of administrative reformers all over the country. . . . "

But in official Washington there were serious doubts and some opposition. The press reported rumors that the Institute planned to undertake a "probe of every branch of government." Senator Lawrence Y. Sherman of Illinois thundered "if any investigating is to be done, it should be through proper legislation. Congress is the proper source of authorization of such a project. If Congress deemed an inquiry necessary, it could direct the executive branch of the government to make it."

Other critics on the Hill were antagonistic to anything that appeared connected with Rockefeller interests, charging that the Institute was a front for attacking the government. Senator Henry F. Ashurst of Arizona voiced his objections to "accepting for government use one cent of Rockefeller money." Despite denials by all parties, the *Washington Times* continued to describe the Institute as a "Rockefeller Inquiry."

The trustees moved carefully to allay suspicions of the Institute's objectives. Some of them had hoped that Cleveland would head the organization, but he was committed to the developing research program of his Bureau. William Willoughby, the Princeton professor who had served on the Rockefeller Foundation's Special Committee on Scientific Research, impressed them with his presence before congressional committees and his knowledge of the Hill, and they realized that these talents would be as important as his recognized scholarship. An experienced public administrator, he had served as Treasurer of Puerto Rico and Assistant Director of the Census before his work on the Taft Commission, and he had just completed two years as constitutional adviser to the Chinese government. In June, he was appointed Director of the Institute.

In the following months, Willoughby worked quietly and effectively to still the initial criticisms. Patiently he explained his objectives to government officials. The Institute's purpose, he emphasized, was to assist them rather than to bring public pressure to bear against them. It was to be truly nonpartisan, he insisted; it would seek no credit for itself.

Meanwhile he worked to recruit his staff. A half dozen senior scholars had been drawn from government and private life by the time the Institute opened its doors on October 2, 1916. Among them were Lewis Meriam, former assistant chief of the Children's Bureau, and Arthur W. Proctor from the New York Bureau of Municipal Research; Henry P. Seidemann, chief clerk of the Bureau of Reclamation; and Gustavus A. Weber, chief of the division of cost of production of the Bureau of Foreign and Domestic Commerce. They were housed in a three-story red brick building at 818 Connecticut Avenue, N.W.

Within weeks, Willoughby's persuasion proved successful: the Bureau of Education, the Federal Farm Loan Board, and the U. S. Employees Compensation Commission requested surveys of their organization, activities, and procedures, and the Bureau of Internal Revenue asked for aid in revising the compilation and reporting of its income and corporation tax statistics.

The Institute also began work on more fundamental

studies, placing highest priority on the need for a national budget system as a necessary first step toward placing the affairs of the government in order. Since this principal recommendation of the Taft Commission had been rejected, the federal government still possessed no budget or adequate system of financial administration. The work Cleveland had directed for the Rockefeller Foundation's Special Committee was turned over to the Institute and published. Willoughby contributed surveys of the movement toward budgetary reform in the states and a major study of the problems involved in developing a national budget. Companion studies sought to describe the practical experience of other governing bodies, and to define desirable principles for government purchasing, accounting, reporting, and personnel administration.

Another priority objective was the assembly of basic facts about the organization, history, and purposes of the major governmental agencies. President Taft had called for such studies in his 1912 message to Congress. "At no time," Taft said, "has the attempt been made to study all of these activities and agencies with a view to the assignment of each activity to the agency best fitted for its performance, to the avoidance of duplication of plant and work, to the integration of all administrative agencies of government, so far as may be practicable, into a unified organization for the most effective and economical dispatch of public business." A series of service monographs was begun to give administrators, members of Congress, and the general public authoritative information on what the government was doing, and to provide comprehensive data for later analysis.

Studies were hardly under way when, in April 1917, war was declared against Germany. The Institute offered its services to the government. The Council of National Defense and the Army Surgeon General's office promptly asked for organizational surveys, and the American Red Cross sought assistance in revising its suddenly overburdened accounting and financial systems. Within a year after its opening, the Institute was fully occupied with wartime work.

Research plans were largely deferred, and much of the staff was dispersed to federal agencies. Financial support became critical as some of the early supporters were unable to fulfill their pledges. Nevertheless, the Institute's wartime services won the confidence of federal agencies and laid a basis for future collaboration of the kind Willoughby had envisioned. And, at this critical period, the Institute's objectives became the personal concern of Robert Brookings.

Brookings was an original in an era of rugged individualists. Born in Cecil County, Maryland, in 1850, he left school at 16, took bookkeeping instruction in Baltimore for several months, and headed west to join his older brother in the St. Louis firm of Cupples and Marston, manufacturers and distributors of woodenware and cordage. His business talents were soon recognized: after a year of clerking he was made a traveling salesman at 18. At 21, he was invited to become a partner in the firm. Before he was 30 he had acquired a fortune, had become the principal management force in the company, and had extended his interests to timber and mining.

Deeply conscious of his own lack of formal education, Brookings sought every opportunity to develop his mind and his taste for the arts and humanities. He became prominent in St. Louis social and civic life. Influenced by Mr. Cupples' philanthropic concerns, he began to consider "the best ways and means of using our surplus for the benefit of humanity." In 1880, touring Europe, he and Cupples studied social services in the London slums. Increasingly he felt a need to devote his growing fortune to public service, until in 1896, at 46, he made his decision. He would retire from business and give the rest of his life to the cause of education.

Cupples was a trustee of Washington University, a failing institution of less than a hundred local students. Brookings was appointed president of the board, and set about building it into a major university. He planned a new campus and raised a substantial endowment for it, contributing much of his own fortune.

Brookings' labors for the University did not keep him from broader national service. In 1910 he became one of the original trustees of the Carnegie Endowment for International Peace. President Taft asked him to serve as a consultant to the Commission on Economy and Efficiency in 1911. The defeat of the Commission's recommendations strengthened his own conviction of the need for federal budgetary and organizational reforms, and he willingly agreed to join the IGR's founding group in 1915, adding his own pledge for $5,000 and raising an additional amount from friends in St. Louis.

In 1917, President Wilson asked him to come to Washington to assist in organizing the War Industries Board. At 67, he threw himself into the emergency with an energy that exhausted younger men. Bernard Baruch had charge of raw materials, Robert A. Lovett was responsible for priorities, and Brookings dealt with finished products. When Baruch later became Chairman of the Board, Brookings was appointed Chairman of the Price Fixing Committee, reporting directly to Wilson. In this post, he was responsible for determining what the Allied governments should pay for all war purchases in the United States—a volume of business that aggregated nearly $30 billion. These tasks challenged his business skills, gave him new insight into the complex relationships developing between the government and the private economy, and convinced him of the need for better data about the government and the economy as a basis for decision-making.

By his presence in Washington he was drawn more deeply into the affairs of the Institute, as other members of the executive committee were scattered in wartime service. By January 1919, only a few thousand dollars remained from the subscriptions and pledges that had underwritten the first years of operations. The trustees asked him to assume the chairmanship.

Brookings was unwilling to see the Institute fail. He wound up the business of his Price Fixing Committee and returned to St. Louis only temporarily. "I am going back to Washington," he told his associates, "to do a bigger piece of work than I have ever done in my life."

He raised $29,000 of the Institute's $36,000 total income for 1919. With financial disaster temporarily averted, he applied his talents of salesmanship to the cause of budget reform. An educator who succumbed to his powers of persuasion once described him as "a benign human steam engine." The engine now rolled over Capitol Hill, persuading the leaders of the House to establish a special Select Committee on the Budget.

The climate for reform was changing. A growing federal debt was stimulating new interest in controlling expenditures and placing government finances on a sound basis. Willoughby's *Problem of a National Budget*, published in 1918, had defined the need. It and other IGR studies provided invaluable guidance for the Select Committee's inquiry. James W. Good, Chairman of the House Committee on Appropriations, asked Willoughby to draft a budget bill, which he introduced intact. Willoughby presented key testimony, suggested other witnesses, and drafted the Committee's report. The House passed the bill with only minor changes. In the Senate, Willoughby played a similar role.

The final result, the Budget and Accounting Act of 1921, was described by President Harding as "the beginning of the greatest reform in governmental practices since the beginning of the republic." It accomplished three fundamental improvements: placing government finance on a budget basis, creating the Bureau of the Budget as a special agency to help the President prepare and administer the budget for the federal government, and establishing an office of Comptroller General as an independent check on the legality of executive expenditures and a source of information for Congress. Further, by giving the President more effective control over the Executive branch, the legislation had a profound impact on the institution of the Presidency.

Meanwhile the Institute staff had been conducting the detailed studies needed to put the budget into operation. When Charles G. Dawes came to Washington as the first Budget Director, he maintained his office for a time at IGR, where he called on the staff for help in determining the form of the budget, installing proper accounting procedures, and working out many of the technical questions involved in inaugurating the new system. Willoughby loaned Dawes a team of IGR technicians headed by Henry Seidemann. Dawes said later that their efforts determined "the whole form of the new budget, of all the general tables setting forth the condition of the treasury, financial operations in the past, and estimates for the future."

Seidemann was largely responsible for the presentation of the budget in 1921 and again in 1922. His staff prepared the summary and analytical tables and contributed an important innovation: a statement of government expenditures for the previous ten years classified by function. He also wrote a *Manual of Accounting and Reporting for the Operating Services of the National Government* (1926) which the General Accounting Office adopted for use in standardizing classification of expenditures by objects, marking an important step toward a uniform accounting system. The Institute helped install the classification system and worked closely with government agencies to assure uniform data, planning, and control.

Robert Somers Brookings
1850–1932

If we can stimulate men to think through these questions of law and government and economics and social relations, we shall do more good to humanity than all the charities.

The young organization was making an impact on Washington in other ways. Lewis Meriam's 1918 treatise on *Principles Governing the Retirement of Public Employees* helped crystallize congressional sentiment in favor of the contributory civil service retirement system which was established in 1920. Lewis Mayer's *The Federal Service: A Study of the System of Personnel Administration of the United States Government*, issued in 1922, made the first detailed analysis of needs for improving the system.

As legislation progressed in Congress, Meriam played a role similar to that Willoughby had played in the field of budgeting. He served as the statistician for the Congressional Joint Committee on Reclassification of Salaries, testified at hearings, and helped draft the measure which, as the Classification Act of 1923, made landmark improvements in the civil service system and salary structure. Later he helped implement the act as an adviser to the Personnel Classification Board which it established. Pioneering work on the preparation and standardization of civil service examinations was also conducted by the Rockefeller-financed Bureau of Public Personnel Administration, directed by Willoughby and housed at the Institute during 1922.

The monograph series early fulfilled its expectations of usefulness. The first two volumes, on the Geological Survey and the Reclamation Service, were issued in 1919; nine more had been published by 1922, and over fifty others had been scheduled.

Work also proceeded on a series of studies of administration. Willoughby's *Reorganization of the Administrative Branch of the National Government*, issued in 1923, called for sweeping changes to meet postwar responsibilities. The volume was used by the Joint Committee on Reorganization as a basis for its consideration of the subject the following year, although no substantial reforms resulted until the next decade. Laurence F. Schmeckebier's *The Statistical Work of the National Government* (1925) laid the groundwork for development of the Central Statistical Board which later became the Office of Statistical Standards in the Budget Bureau.

As the young Institute added to its accomplishments other distinguished men joined its Board of Trustees: among them Herbert Hoover, Elihu Root, and Chief Justice William Howard Taft. Nevertheless financing continued to be an acute problem. By 1920 funds were again exhausted, and Brookings assumed responsibility for raising a sustaining fund for a second five-year period.

At 70, the old traveling salesman once more took to the road. In major cities throughout the country—Boston, Pittsburgh, Chicago, New York, Philadelphia, Cleveland, Youngstown, St. Louis—Brookings met with leading citizens and businessmen to enlist their support for the work of the Institute. "You see how the government is spending the money it takes from you in taxes. What are you going to do about it?" he asked them. "Do you want an intelligent treatment of the matters which lie closest to your personal interests? Or do you want things to go on in the haphazard fashion of the past? Do you want a log-rolling or a scientific tariff? Do you want pork-barrel bills or a budget?"

In two months, he returned with subscriptions totaling $324,550 from ninety-two corporations and twelve individuals. The continued existence of the Institute was assured, but the strain convinced Brookings that the organization could not be financed in this way indefinitely. He began to seek long-term support from the major philanthropic foundations.

Brookings also saw that the Institute was merely scratching the surface of the problems facing the nation. His wartime experiences had shown him that basic economic data were just as vitally needed for intelligent decision-making as administrative facts, and were practically nonexistent. He found that other leaders in business, education, and government shared his views, and he took the lead in organizing another institute, designed to do for economic policy what the Institute for Government Research was doing for government administration.

He called on his friend Henry Pritchett, President of the Carnegie Corporation, who later recalled the impression Brookings had made: "He laid before me in complete and concrete form the conception of an institute of economics which others had in a vague way hinted at. I lost no time in laying his proposal before the Board." On January 5, 1922, Brookings submitted a formal request for a ten-year sustaining grant of $1,650,000 to found an Institute of Economics.

"The events of the past ten years, and particularly those of the years since the War, have gone far to emphasize the fact that many governmental questions are, in their essence, economic questions," the proposal declared. "It is clear today to thinking men that the basis upon which just settlements must be made as between groups of citizens and as between nations must be economic." A nonpartisan agency was proposed to "collect, interpret, and lay before the country in clear and intelligible form the fundamental economic facts concerning which opinions need to be formed." Eighteen other distinguished Americans joined Brookings in signing the proposal.

The Carnegie Corporation agreed to make the grant, contributing $200,000 a year for five years, with the balance tapering off in the second five-year period. The Institute was chartered on February 13, 1922. Dr. Pritchett and several of the Carnegie trustees participated in the meeting which formally organized the Institute on April 21. Brookings was unanimously elected President of a Board of Trustees which included Alderman, Hadley, Lowell, and Mather from the IGR Board; Whitefoord R. Cole, president of the Louisville and Nashville Railroad; David F. Houston, Chairman of the Board of the Mutual Life Insurance Company who had served as Secretary of Agriculture and Secretary of the Treasury; Charles L. Hutchinson, former President of the Corn Exchange Bank of Chicago; David Kinley, President of the University of Illinois; John Barton Payne, Chairman of the American Red Cross; Memphis investment banker Bolton Smith; New York banker James J. Storrow; Associate Supreme Court Justice George Sutherland; Charles D. Walcott, Secretary of the Smithsonian Institution; and banker Paul M. Warburg.

To direct the new Institute, the trustees selected Harold Glenn Moulton, professor of political economy at the University of Chicago. At 39, he was already recognized as an outstanding young economist. One of his early volumes had broken new ground in explaining the role of banking and finance in the economy, another on the financial organization of society had achieved wide acceptance as a university text, and he had just published a timely study of war debts and the problem of their adjustment.

When he was asked to accept the directorship Moulton was doubtful. Brookings' enthusiasm for the potentialities of economics aroused the suspicions of a scholar who knew that it was not an exact science. Wary that Brookings might try to use the Institute as a vehicle for his own amateurish economic theories, Moulton demurred: he was not interested, he said, if the organization was to be the mouthpiece of any one man or group of men. The older man assured him that he and his staff would have a free hand, but at Moulton's insistence the by-laws provided "that the primary function of the trustees is not to express their views on the scientific investigations conducted by the Institute, but only to make it possible for such scientific work to be done under the most favorable auspices."

In June 1922, the Institute began operations in temporary quarters at the American National Bank Building, Brookings' own suite of offices, until completion of an eight-story building he had erected to bring both his Institutes under the same roof. The new quarters at 26 (later 744) Jackson Place were occupied in early

September, when the Institute of Economics took over the top two floors and the IGR moved over from Connecticut Avenue. They shared a library and conference rooms in the basement, and the remaining space was rented to the American Council on Education and several other nonprofit organizations.

Moulton laid out a program of research in four main fields: international economic reconstruction, international commercial policies, agriculture, and industry and labor. Unlike the early days of the IGR, there was no need to persuade official Washington of the need for such studies. Calls for consultation and staff assistance came readily from Congress, the Tariff Commission, state officials, and industry. To begin the work, a dozen senior economists were assembled. Among them were Edwin G. Nourse, chief of agricultural economics at Iowa State College; Thomas Walker Page, vice president of the American Economic Association and former chairman of the Tariff Commission; Leo Pasvolsky, a young economist and free lance writer; and Isador Lubin, a University of Michigan economist formerly on the staff of the War Industries Board.

Moulton had early recognized that the reparations obligations and interallied war debts seriously clouded the outlook for world economic recovery. His own studies and those of other staff members drew attention to these problems and notably influenced the readjustment of international debt policies. In *Germany's Capacity to Pay* (1923), he differentiated between the problems of internal collection and the problems of transfer abroad, concluding that existing reparations policies were undermining the German economy, and that changes were urgently needed to aid recovery of its import and export trade. His analysis was closely studied by the international Dawes Committee. One of the British delegates, Sir Josiah Stamp, later recalled that the book was the only comprehensive assembly of facts and interpretation the committee had: since its conclusions were unacceptable to expectant creditors, however, he refrained from quoting from it openly, keeping his copy in a drawer for ready reference.

Other staff studies built on Moulton's work. An analysis of the French debt problem led to a scaling down of claims on France by the United States government, much to the chagrin of Secretary of Commerce Hoover, who told a press conference that Moulton represented a liability to the United States to the extent of $10 million a year in perpetuity. (Years later, however, President Hoover found it necessary to declare a moratorium on all intergovernmental war debts.) Later studies in this series furnished a basis for settlement of Russian, Italian, Bulgarian, and Danubian war debts, and stated general principles about the nature of international obligations which contributed to a better understanding of the problem. *The International Accounts*, by Cleona Lewis (1927), made recommendations for standardized reporting of international financial statements which were substantially adopted by the League of Nations.

A second series of projects focused on tariff studies under the direction of Thomas Walker Page. The high tariff wall raised by the Harding Administration was one of the chief obstacles to international economic recovery. In 1922, duties had been raised to unprecedented heights, thus handicapping European nations in their efforts to sell goods in the United States. Now, in a series of studies of sugar, wool, livestock, and other industries, the Institute demonstrated the restrictive effects of the tariff on the U. S. economy. The Smoot-Hawley tariff of 1930 imposed even higher duties, leading to retaliatory foreign tariffs against American goods, but the Institute's work helped lay the factual groundwork for comprehensive changes in tariff policy embodied in the Reciprocal Trade Agreements Act of 1934.

Studies of agriculture by Edwin G. Nourse and others examined the causes of the decline in farm prices which set in following World War I. Nourse, who served as President of the American Farm Economic Association in 1925, showed that there was no hope that European recovery would rescue the domestic market. Pointing to the need for improvement of farm management and marketing, he assessed the potentialities of rural credit institutions and other new forms of economic organization then evolving in American agriculture. While Nourse examined the ills of agriculture, Lubin and others focused early attention on unemployment problems, with special emphasis on the growing economic plight of the coal industry.

Robert Brookings continued to serve as President of the Corporation of Washington University. In 1923, he endowed a graduate department of economics and government with a unique feature: doctoral students were to divide their time between St. Louis and Washington, where they would work on practical problems of government in association with the staffs of the two Institutes. Brookings purchased an old private home at 1724 Eye Street as a Washington residence for the students, and pledged annual support for twenty fellowships of $1,000 each.

By the time the first class was enrolled in the fall of 1924, it was evident that the Washington operation should have an independent existence. Its remoteness from the University in St. Louis not only complicated its management but jeopardized the University's tax exemption under the laws of Missouri. Accordingly, the University trustees granted independence and arranged for an appropriate transfer of funds and property. The new institution was then incorporated in the District of Columbia on November 24, 1924, as the Robert Brookings Graduate School of Economics and Government.

The school's Board of Trustees was headed by Brookings and included Goodnow and Greene from the IGR board; Moulton, Frederic A. Delano of the Federal Reserve Board; George Eastman of the Eastman Kodak Company; and four trustees of the Institute of Economics: Walcott; Vernon L. Kellogg, Permanent Secretary of the National Research Council; John C. Merriam, President of the Carnegie Institution of Washington; and Leo S. Rowe, Director General of the Pan American Union. Financially, the school began on a sound footing: Brookings pledged capital funds to yield an income of $44,000 a year, and Eastman pledged $50,000 a year for seven years. Miss Isabel Vallé

January, a long-time friend who shared Brookings' civic interests in St. Louis, and who was to become his wife in 1927, pledged $350,000.

Moulton was appointed vice president and chief administrative officer of the school. The thirty-seven students attending in the first year were taught by a small faculty of teacher-scholars including Walton H. Hamilton from Amherst, Walter J. Shepard from Ohio State University, and Leverett S. Lyon from the University of Chicago. Moulton, Nourse, Willoughby, Helen Wright, and other staff members of the Institutes assisted with instruction, and leading university scholars and government officials participated as occasional lecturers and discussion leaders.

Frankly experimental in nature, reflecting Brookings' personal views of the inadequacies of most graduate education, the school soon attracted wide attention for its innovations and its pioneering emphasis on training for the public service. Its doctoral program placed primary emphasis on the opportunities afforded for ready access to the source materials of public policy research and personal contact and discussion with Washington officials. Studies focused on the larger economic and political questions of contemporary culture rather than on the academic disciplines. There were no formal courses, credits, majors, or minors: students were expected to participate in a series of short seminars, undertake extensive readings, and work on practical problems of government policy with the staff of the Institutes.

Authorities in various fields were invited to take up residence as faculty associates for brief periods and make themselves available for individual consultation. In successive days or weeks students might hear Carl Becker or Charles A. Beard discourse on the nature of history, Roscoe Pound on systems of jurisprudence, Lewis Mumford on American literary criticism, or Stanley K. Hornbeck on the economy of China. Another week might bring discussions with Alvin Johnson, Felix Frankfurter, Harold Laski, George Boas, or Alexander Meiklejohn.

This heady intellectual atmosphere nurtured some 120 Fellows, many of whom later distinguished themselves in public service, research, and education. Seventy-four were awarded the Ph.D. degree, among them Mordecai Ezekiel, George B. Galloway, Paul T. Homan, Lewis Webster Jones, Dexter M. Keezer, Max Lerner, Stacy May, John U. Nef, Winfield W. Riefler, Carl B. Swisher, George W. Terborgh, and Woodlief Thomas.

Students came from universities across the country, but the bright promise of the Graduate School was never fully realized. Within four years of its founding, it was abolished as a degree-granting institution. Its facilities and research training functions were merged with those of the two Institutes to establish the Brookings Institution. Before the change was accomplished, the role of the school became a subject of bitter controversy and a public *cause célèbre*.

The difficulties were partly due to the school's success, which caused a deepening division between faculty and administration over its primary mission. From the beginning, Brookings had viewed it primarily as an agency to train persons for public service and policy research—a function he considered more important than any formal status as an academic institution. The principal purpose of the school, he declared, was "to teach the art of handling problems rather than to impart accumulated knowledge; and its end is to turn out craftsmen who can make contributions to an intelligent direction of social change." His own experience in government and at the Institutes had shown him that such craftsmen were scarce.

As early as 1924, he had considered merging all three institutions into one permanent organization devoted to a wider range of activities, and he established overlapping membership among the trustees to facilitate an eventual merger. The following year, he asked the executive committees of each institution to prepare a plan of consolidation.

As their plans proceeded, the dean of the faculty, Walton Hamilton, entered a strong dissent. Whereas Brookings saw the school as an experiment in training for public service, Hamilton viewed it as an experiment in graduate education. A brilliant teacher, he saw its location in Washington and its association with the Institutes as opening possibilities for a distinctively personal kind of graduate education with a potential for far-reaching influence on university instruction. In its brief lifetime, the school had already demonstrated his case, he argued: therefore it should retain an autonomous identity and should not be made subservient to a larger institution. Its student body necessarily differentiated it from a research organization; outstanding teachers could not necessarily be obtained by hiring outstanding researchers.

Brookings fully recognized the possibilities which Hamilton's genius had demonstrated, but felt that continued independence would inevitably lead to greater emphasis on training for academic pursuits than for the practical life of public affairs. He had no intention of allowing the school to duplicate the work of other graduate institutions.

"I have become convinced," he wrote Hamilton, "that the granting of a doctor's degree has had a tendency to bring us less mature students . . . who have had primarily in mind a teaching career, the universities of the country having made such a degree almost an ultimatum in their teaching requirements. Frankly, while of course we all admit the value . . . which might be rendered by our graduates (by an improved teaching service), it is a long way in its results from the direct service I have always had in mind, and the necessity for which has grown upon me every year."

Hamilton was supported by his faculty and students. In the summer of 1927, Brookings turned to Abraham Flexner of the General Education Board for advice, and Flexner spent two weeks investigating conditions at the school. His first reaction was that the faculty of "three men and a girl" was hopelessly inadequate, but he finally refused to submit any recommendations. Apologetically, he wrote Brookings that "the field is so far from anything with which I have had practical experience and knowledge, and the actual facts are so weighty

—namely, the existence of three separate institutions, each guided by a different personality—that I cannot undertake to advise as to the type of reorganization that would most effectively accomplish the objects for which the three institutions were established. One cannot be an authority in many fields, and this field I am reluctantly driven to conclude is one in which it would not be right for me to form an opinion."

On December 8, 1927, the boards of trustees of the three institutions met jointly and unanimously approved consolidation. The Brookings Institution was chartered "to promote, carry on, conduct and foster scientific research, education, training and publication in the broad fields of economics, government administration and the political and social sciences generally, involving the study, determination, interpretation and publication of economic, political and social facts and principles relating to questions of local, national or international significance; to promote and carry out these objects, purposes and principles without regard to and independently of the special interests of any group in the body politic, either political, social or economic."

The trustees were responsible for management of the Institution's finances, approval of major fields of investigation, and the maintenance of scientific standards. But "it is not part of their function," the by-laws stated, "to determine, control, or influence the conduct of particular investigations or the conclusions reached."

The faculty of the school were assured a place on the staff, but Hamilton resigned, and his outraged students took up his banner. For a time the controversy livened the pages of national magazines. Two former students wrote an article charging that the abolition of the school was hasty and ill conceived, that the faculty were not consulted, and that the step was a serious loss for American graduate education. Moulton replied in defense of the amalgamation. Then Charles A. Beard took to print to charge that Moulton's defense was inadequate. Moulton invited him to make a personal investigation of the facts, which resulted in Beard's finding that consolidation was made with the full knowledge and active leadership of Mr. Brookings "with a view to realizing more perfectly his original ideas respecting the Graduate School by relating the teaching of higher graduate students more vitally to the realism of the research work . . . ."

The consolidated Institution was organized July 1, 1928. Brookings, now seventy-eight, was Chairman of the board. Six other trustees remained from the original founding group of 1914–1916: Edwin A. Alderman, Raymond Fosdick, Frank J. Goodnow, Jerome D. Greene, Arthur T. Hadley, and Samuel Mather. The rest of the board included Whiteford R. Cole, Frederic A. Delano, George Eastman, Ernest M. Hopkins, David F. Houston, Vernon L. Kellogg, John C. Merriam, Harold G. Moulton, John Barton Payne, Leo S. Rowe, Bolton Smith, and Paul M. Warburg. Moulton, who had earned wide respect and recognition for the Institute of Economics, borne the chief administrative burdens of the Graduate School, and directed the planning for consolidation, was elected first President of the Institution.

Announcement of the consolidation received respect-
ful attention in the nation's press. The *Philadelphia
Public Ledger* declared that the new Institution "may be
regarded, in a sense, as a Christmas gift to the country,
for its benefits will be freely available and far-reaching."
The *Washington Post* predicted that the Institution
"probably will sweep swiftly to the front in leadership
in this branch of intellectual activity." The *Kansas City
Star*, joining in editorial praise, argued the value of
social science research with greater hindsight than fore-
sight: "It is needless to dwell on the importance of
economic and political research. Secretary Hoover's
great success in promoting the industrial welfare of the
country has come largely from the systematized information his department has gathered."

III

THE THIRTIES

Depression and Controversy

[Brookings] publications cause something of a stir in the world. Newspapers print summaries of them on their front pages. Economists, editorial writers and some politicians cite them much as Fundamentalist preachers draw upon Holy Writ. Although the emotional appeal of these books is nil, their statements have caused many highly placed or otherwise prominent persons to yell bloody murder.

THE NEW YORK TIMES, MARCH 20, 1938

To HAROLD MOULTON, the Institution was more than a union of the three existing organizations. He assumed charge with the expressed intention of enlarging their activities and broadening their objectives. He envisioned a comprehensive social science center promoting organized research and training in all the humanistic sciences; playing a constructive and practical role in the solution of economic, social, and political problems; serving as a center for visiting scholars; and fostering policy research in the country at large.

The two Institutes had now become operating divisions, and additional institutes representing other social science disciplines were projected. The Graduate School had become the Training Division, with a supergraduate program replacing the earlier doctoral program.

The new Institution, Moulton hoped, would help revitalize the social sciences by breaking down the artificial barriers that had grown up between the various disciplines. He quoted trustee Raymond Fosdick:

Unless we can marshal behind such studies as economics, political science, and sociology the same enthusiasm, the same approach and something of the same technique that characterize our treatment of physics and chemistry; unless the results

43

of this research can be applied to human life as freely and boldly as we apply the natural sciences to modify our methods of living; unless we can free ourselves of prejudice and stale custom and harness intelligence to the task of straightening out the relations of man with his fellowmen and promoting an intercourse of harmony and fairness—unless, in brief, in our generation we can make some appreciable progress toward this goal of social control, then pessimism has the better of the argument, and the chances of our keeping the train on the track are exceedingly slight.

The IGR had already begun to broaden its interests. Administrative reform at the state level became a subject of concern in 1924, when the Government of Hawaii requested help in revising its financial structure. Henry Seidemann established a model budget system which was enacted by the Territorial legislature, and supervised its installation. Several state governments asked for assistance in drafting personnel and accounting procedures.

Studies of the national government focused increasingly on policy questions as well as administrative matters. The service monograph series, which by 1927 already numbered over fifty volumes, reflected this shift. Some of the administrative policy issues identified in the earlier statistical studies were subjected to further analysis.

Willoughby initiated new investigations of the federal regulatory agencies, and of the problems of federal-state coordination. His *Principles of Public Administration*, published in 1927, provided one of the first texts in this field and marked the culmination of the program of work he had laid out a decade earlier. In *Principles of Judicial Administration*, published in 1929, he highlighted the growing problem of governmental encroachment on individual liberties and examined the increasing authority of the Executive branch which challenged traditional concepts of the distribution of governmental powers.

A study of Indian affairs, directed by Meriam and made at the request of Secretary of the Interior Hubert Work, revealed the wretched condition of the Indians and recommended a comprehensive educational program emphasizing health, advancement of productive efficiency, and higher standards of family and community life. Published in 1929, the report called for greatly enlarged expenditures, and reversal of federal policies that had tended to pauperize the Indians. Its findings led directly to professionalization of the Bureau of Indian Affairs and other such fundamental reforms of policy and administration that the report became known as the "Bible of the Indian Service."

The Institute of Economics had evidenced its concern for policy problems from the beginning. Now Moulton turned its directorship over to Edwin G. Nourse, whose earlier work had focused attention on issues of agricultural marketing and rural credit policy. In the latter years of the decade, the influential series of war debt and tariff studies was completed.

A six-year study of the St. Lawrence Seaway proposal, published in 1929, caused more anguish for Herbert Hoover: his new administration had urged adoption of the project, as had each administration since the war. Now, the Brookings analysis found cost estimates to be five times higher than the government's, and the Seaway was doomed to congressional defeat.

The Institute undertook new inquiries into the growing problems of the domestic economy. With *Cooperative Marketing of Livestock*, Nourse began studies of the Federal Farm Board experiment which led to a major examination of the Agricultural Adjustment Administration several years later. Lubin's *Absorption of the Unemployed by American Industry* (1929), and other staff studies of unemployment insurance in Germany and the British attack on unemployment, reflected the Institute's early awareness of issues that were to be the subject of national legislation in the Employment Act of 1946.

With the abolition of the Graduate School, Leverett S. Lyon directed its transformation into a Training Division. The Institution's commitments to the students in residence were fulfilled, and the last class of Ph.D.'s was graduated in 1930. From 1928 on, predoctoral and postdoctoral fellows were appointed annually. They participated in seminars, worked with the staffs of the research divisions, and took their degrees at their home institutions.

Plans were drawn to bring the three institutions together physically in a single headquarters. In 1929, a site at 722 Jackson Place was obtained, and work began on a new building with funds contributed by Mrs. Brookings in memory of her mother, Grace Vallé January.

The new structure was dedicated May 15, 1931. The

founder, in poor health at 81, was unable to attend the ceremonies, but his old colleague Jerome Greene was present to pay tribute to the Institution's growing role in Washington. The eight-story limestone edifice was, in truth, a physical reminder of this role: it stood as a significant landmark facing Lafayette Square, diagonally across the park from the White House and the Treasury, a half block from the old State-War-Navy Building (now the Executive Office Building) on one side and the U. S. Chamber of Commerce on the other.

Fronting on the square were ample offices for the research and administrative staffs, a well-equipped library, conference rooms, and publications office. Behind it, connected by an enclosed arcade with a formal court, were the club-like quarters of the residence building. In the first-floor lounge, a lengthy room with oak-paneled walls, baronial fireplace and beamed ceiling, scholars, fellows, and guests mingled socially or gathered for lectures and informal talk. In the dining rooms above, theorists daily tested their opinions against the experience of government officials. The private Round Table Room, where off-the-record discussions were held with distinguished guests, was to become a Washington meeting place as celebrated as Bernard Baruch's bench in the park outside (and considerably more comfortable). On the upper floors were dormitory rooms for fellows and visiting scholars, a small gymnasium, and the best squash court in Washington, where Dr. Moulton regularly defended his unofficial institutional championship.

For all the comfortable appointments of the new

quarters, the dedication predictions that the Institution was entering "a new period of national and international usefulness" were brave but uncertain words, spoken at a time of deepening national depression. Thousands of homes, farms, and businesses had already been lost. As the economy disintegrated, President Hoover appealed to "rugged individualism" and struggled to solve the crisis under the handicap of traditional concepts that held a balanced budget to be the first essential for recovery.

At the Institution, as throughout the country, plans for the future were necessarily deferred or curtailed. The additional institutes which had been envisioned were never brought into being (although Moulton obtained approval in principle for establishment of institutes of international relations, industrial psychology, judicial administration, public finance, and social welfare). An opportunity to affiliate the Municipal Administration Service of New York and broaden it into a general clearing house of information in the field of public administration was lost for lack of funds. Willoughby's hope to found a journal of public administration was abandoned; so was Moulton's plan to produce a series of basic economics texts and other curriculum materials for colleges and secondary schools.

In the spring of 1932, a ragged army of 15,000 bonus marchers camped in the Anacostia flats laid sullen siege to Washington. Farm prices plummeted to their lowest point; in the wheat belt of the Midwest, farmers banded together to fight dispossession, and the head of the Farm Bureau Federation predicted "revolution in the

Isabel Vallé Brookings

1876–1965

countryside in less than twelve months" unless something was done. Nearly a quarter of the labor force was unemployed. Business failures reached an all time high. The Institution's financial resources were close to exhaustion.

The ten-year Carnegie grant which had established the Institute of Economics had been tapering off since 1927, and now it expired. The Corporation informed Moulton that it could not consider further large-scale support. A seven-year grant made by the Laura Spelman Rockefeller Foundation in 1924 to support research in government administration also ran out. The Rockefeller Foundation agreed to provide $2 million for endowment if the Institution could raise matching funds, and Julius Rosenwald pledged half of the needed amount, but the balance could not be raised and the commitment was canceled. George Eastman's support, which had amounted to $50,000 annually since 1925, was terminated with his death in 1932.

Brookings had contributed over $1 million in capital funds for the Institution, but to his deep regret his personal resources were no longer adequate to provide an endowment. "If I only were younger, the Institution wouldn't have to worry about money. I'd make a nuisance of myself till I got it," he said. He now made annual payments to help meet operating expenses. At his death November 15, 1932, the full burden of raising funds for the Institution fell on Moulton.

Mrs. Brookings, as devoted to the Institution as her late husband, continued to make annual contributions. Moulton also sought support from other individuals, but with little success. Unlike the universities, the Institution had no large alumni body to be solicited. The trustees decided not to seek corporate donations, as Mr. Brookings had done in earlier years, in the belief that the Institution could best preserve its reputation for impartiality by remaining independent of all interest groups.

Several years earlier, at a time when most institutional funds were invested in bonds to conserve existing assets, Moulton established guiding principles under which a major percentage of the Institution's slim endowment funds were placed in diversified stock holdings which afforded relatively higher yields and long-term growth. He also made astute use of the Institution's real estate to construct and operate office buildings on its downtown Washington properties, and in later years these brought in a growing rental income. Now, however, income from investments brought in less than 10 percent of a $300,000 annual budget. Improvised financing through project grants and service investigations were the only means of financing available. Using these slim means, Moulton brought the poorly financed Institution through the depression and into one of its most productive periods.

One project which helped keep the Institution solvent in its most crucial year was a major study of transportation policy, carried out under a national committee headed by former President Coolidge. Moulton had been instrumental in calling attention to the need for such a study, and arranged to have himself appointed its director. *The American Transportation Problem*, published in 1933, helped clarify the fundamental issues of transport coordination and control and influenced the improvement of regulatory procedures.

The IGR's pioneering state surveys in the late 1920's now brought welcome requests from other states desperately seeking ways to improve the economy and efficiency of their governmental machinery. North Carolina, Alabama, New Hampshire, Mississippi, Iowa, and Oklahoma came under analysis. The resulting reports introduced improvements in taxation, budgeting, personnel management, procurement, and other aspects of administrative organization and procedure. The Institution's work inspired other similar studies, and marked the beginning of a trend toward badly needed modernization and overhaul of state governments.

Another important new source of support was the Maurice and Laura Falk Foundation of Pittsburgh. In 1932, the young foundation was just beginning to organize a program of philanthropy which was to make significant contributions in economics, education, medicine and culture over three decades until its dissolution in 1965. Its first grant was made to Brookings, to inaugurate a major program of research on the distribution of income and wealth in relation to economic progress. This was followed by a series of grants extending over the lifetime of the foundation and totalling more than $1.5 million for support of the Institution's economic research and for dissemination of its findings.

The Institution was also sustained by the consulting services provided by members of the staff to the Cham-

ber of Commerce, the American Federation of Labor, the National Tax Association, the American Institute of Agricultural Cooperation, and the League of Nations. With a keen sense of public relations, Moulton negotiated a weekly network radio program with the National Advisory Council on Radio in Education, one of the early ventures in public service broadcasting.

The Institution managed to continue its own research. In *War Debts and World Prosperity*, Moulton and Pasvolsky synthesized their earlier work on world debt settlements. Studies of marketing, population problems, federal credit policies, housing, and transportation came from the presses, as well as a theoretical study of statistical trend analysis. Joseph P. Harris, whose *Registration of Voters in the United States* in 1929 drew attention to the deficiencies of election laws and administration, completed a sequel, *Election Administration in the United States*, proposing model procedures which were widely adopted.

Willoughby retired in 1932, capping his distinguished career by serving as president of the American Political Science Association. He was succeeded as Director of IGR by Arnold Bennett Hall, a lawyer and political scientist who had served as president of the University of Oregon. Two years later the Institution issued Willoughby's summary of a lifetime's work, *Principles of Legislative Organization and Administration*, as well as the sixty-sixth and last of the service monographs he had initiated.

Nineteen thirty-three had begun in violence. An unemployed bricklayer attempted to assassinate President-elect Franklin Delano Roosevelt in Miami, spraying his car with bullets from 35 feet away and killing Mayor Cermak of Chicago. Food riots were common, and ugly "Hoovervilles" were rising on the outskirts of the cities. The system of distributing wealth and goods had suffered a monumental breakdown. The nation watched anxiously as the new national administration assumed power.

In the pre-inaugural months, Roosevelt planned sweeping reductions in public expenditures, consolidation of bureaus, and elimination of government functions. In January, he had written to Moulton, "quite frankly, we need help. Because I know of the splendid work that has been done by you and the Institute, and because of my old friendship for Mr. Brookings, I am hoping that you will be able to give us assistance in the preparation of a fairly definite plan between now and early March." Several memoranda outlining suggested economies were submitted to Roosevelt's staff, and Henry Seidemann prepared detailed plans for completing his work on budget reforms for the guidance of the new Budget Director, Lewis Douglas.

The proposals were never adopted, for Roosevelt once in office took a different tack, calling for "bold, persistent experimentation." In his first hundred days, a course of vigorous governmental action was charted. Across America, people began to take new hope. But at Brookings, the reaction was skeptical.

Moulton and other members of the staff expressed concern over the implications of a central federal role in the economy. Charles O. Hardy wrote that the aim of the New Deal legislation was "to substitute centralized authority of one sort or another for what is left of free competitive enterprise." When Roosevelt signed the National Recovery Act, calling it probably "the most important and far-reaching legislation ever enacted by the American Congress," Moulton pointed out that "its major purpose is to control or influence the organization and functioning of business in general," and that it was "certain to modify the structure and the functioning of many of our economic institutions and leave them changed when the period of emergency has passed." He announced that the Institution would appraise the effects of two principal New Deal agencies, the National Recovery Administration and the Agricultural Adjustment Administration, in a series of major investigations. Supported by the Rockefeller Foundation, they were based on Nourse's concern for capture-and-record studies of "concurrent history."

Though sometimes hostile, the studies were useful to the government. After reading George Terborgh's Brookings report on price control devices in the NRA codes, Roosevelt appointed a Cabinet committee under Frances Perkins to consider the long-run implications of price policies.

Terborgh's work was part of a five-part examination of NRA operations and their social and economic consequences. The NRA series, directed by Leverett S. Lyon, pointed to critical deficiencies in the administration of the agency and the operation of its industry codes. While he and a staff gathered material, Lyon served as Deputy NRA Administrator for Policy on Trade Practices. Their findings indicated that the administration of the act had broken down, and that it could not achieve its objectives.

When galley proofs of the final report were made available to the Senate Finance Committee's investigation of the agency in early 1935, cries of outrage issued from General Hugh S. Johnson, NRA Administrator. The Institution, he charged, had become "a pressure bureau to publicize the preconceived ideas of Harold Moulton."

Johnson had been associated with Robert Brookings on the War Production Board two decades earlier. Now, he complained, the Institution was "masquerading under the ideas of its grand old founder . . . . I wish Robert Brookings were here today. He would go into that Institution that bears his name and drive out with the rope around his robe the men who perverted his ideas." He scoffed at the findings of the NRA report: "Before anybody asks that crowd for a prescription he must write his own diagnosis. It is one of the most sanctimonious and pontifical rackets in the country."

But the NRA was already in trouble within the administration: discontent with the codes was so great that Roosevelt had set up a special review board under Clarence Darrow. He reported that the codes had failed as an experiment in business self-government. Largely drafted by industry, the codes had encouraged "bold and aggressive monopolistic practices" permitting the most powerful interests to seize control of entire industries. Before Congress reached a decision on the agency's future, the Supreme Court declared the National Recovery Act unconstitutional.

Others in the administration besides Johnson had

little use for the Institution. Its traditional interest in technical administrative reform did not appeal to administrators engrossed in the New Deal's pragmatic search for positive action: many shared the view of Harry Hopkins, who curtly told a Budget Bureau inspector seeking an organizational chart of his relief program, "I don't want anybody around here to waste any time drawing boxes."

But others in government found the Institution's critical analysis helpful. Secretary of Agriculture Henry A. Wallace readily assented to Nourse's plans for a comprehensive study of the AAA. "We've been doing so much wishful thinking around here, we'd benefit from an independent audit," he declared.

The resulting studies, directed by Nourse, criticized the agency's production control devices but cleared it of charges that benefit payments to farmers had been politically manipulated. The AAA was found to be generally sound as originally conceived, and desirable as an emergency measure. Secretary Wallace wrote Nourse and his associates that he disagreed with some of their conclusions, but that they had "unquestionably performed a valuable service" with their commodity studies, particularly their final summary volume, *Three Years of the Agricultural Adjustment Administration.*

As the powerful initiatives of the New Deal continued, relations cooled between Moulton and the White House. When Roosevelt set up his Committee on Administrative Management under Louis Brownlow, the President vetoed a place for Moulton on the distinguished committee. In Congress, leaders of the anti-

Roosevelt movement pushed through authorization for a coordinate investigation headed by Harry F. Byrd in the Senate and J. P. Buchanan in the House. They turned to Moulton and his staff for a report on administrative overlapping and duplication in the federal departments.

The two studies were intended to complement each other, with Brookings covering questions of allocation of functions within and among departments and the Brownlow Committee taking up the broader questions of administrative management related to the President's function as chief executive. Funds were in fact assigned by the Brownlow Committee to support the Brookings survey. On certain points where the two studies over-lapped, however—particularly the settlement functions of the Comptroller General and the status and functions of the independent commissions—they were in disagreement. On these points, the Brookings group tended to oppose the expansion of Executive control over the regulatory functions which the Brownlow Committee advocated.

Another Brookings study of compulsory health insurance for the Senate Committee on Labor and Public Welfare questioned the need for a national program, supplying factual ammunition for the successful fight to keep health insurance out of the original social security legislation. Such aid and comfort to the anti-New Deal forces drew the wrath of Roosevelt's brain trusters. Rexford Guy Tugwell belittled the Institution as "a kind of research organ for the conservatives."

Moulton enjoyed the intellectual contest. He hit back at his attackers in speeches and pamphlets, pointing out that: "Such attacks have been made both by members of Congress and by administrative officials of Republican as well as Democratic regimes. In the main, however, the investigations of the Institution have been welcomed as thorough analyses and interpretations of important issues, and hence worthy of careful study by everyone interested in economic and governmental progress." He was careful to make its findings available on a nonpartisan basis. He periodically addressed letters to all members of Congress, calling attention to recent studies and offering to supply copies without charge on written request.

His personal differences of opinion with the administration were not shared by many staff members, notably Nourse, who took a more tolerant attitude toward the innovations of the administration. In the foreword to his AAA study, he asserted that: "A social agency, like a mechanical device, may be safe and useful in one man's hands or in certain circumstances and an engine of destruction as used by another or in other circumstances."

In any case, Moulton's opposition to New Deal measures did not interfere with the demand for staff services. Henry Seidemann was loaned to the AAA to devise its complicated procedures for paying agricultural benefits. With the passage of the Social Security Act in 1935, he designed and organized the enormous accounting and control system for payroll taxes and benefit payments, and later served as Director of the Bureau of Old Age Benefits. Harold Rowe went to the Department of Agriculture on temporary assignment as assistant to Secretary Wallace to appraise the AAA program; Isador Lubin was appointed Commissioner of Labor Statistics, and Leo Pasvolsky went to the Department of State as assistant to Secretary Cordell Hull. Some of the Institution's trustees during the decade served prominently in the administration: Frederic A. Delano, who became Chairman of the Board following the death of Mr. Brookings, headed the National Resources Planning Board; John G. Winant was Chairman of the Social Security Board; Norman H. Davis headed U. S. delegations to the Geneva Disarmament Conference, the London Naval Conference, and the Brussels Nine Power Conference.

The Institute of Economics under Nourse was winning wide respect. It was, said the *New York Times*, "as important in the world of economic research as the Pasteur Institute is in the world of medicine." As the decade wore on, its research on the relation of income distribution to economic progress influenced economic thinking in and out of government and foreshadowed a major thesis of the "new economics" of today by emphasizing the need to match America's capacity to consume with its capacity to produce.

Four volumes were published in this series, which Walter Lippmann described as "the most useful economic study made in America during the depression." *America's Capacity to Produce*, by Nourse and associates, and *America's Capacity to Consume*, by Maurice Leven, Moulton, and Clark Warburton, appeared in 1934. In the following year Moulton issued his *The Formation of Capital* and *Income and Economic Progress*. Together the studies argued the need for passing on a large part of the gains of technical progress to the whole population through lower prices. Refuting the view that the United States economy had reached stagnation, they forecast the prospect of a dynamic economy based on the increased output which would result from technical advances and from the expansion of consumer demand stimulated by lower prices and wider distribution of national income.

Within the government a survey was launched to determine the pattern of expenditures at different income levels, the relation of income concentration to personal savings, and the expansibility of consumer demand with rising incomes. The failure of NRA, the onset of another recession in 1937, and other developments led to a redirection of policies, and greater emphasis was placed on improving the price-wage ratio as a primary requirement for expanding demand.

As economists and political scientists worked together on Brookings projects, the line of demarcation between the research divisions became less distinct. On the death of Arnold Hall in 1936, Fred Wilbur Powell, a member of the senior staff since 1920, was appointed Acting Director of IGR. When illness forced his own resignation the following year, the directorship became largely honorific, rotating annually among Meriam, Seidemann, and Schmeckebier.

By 1938, some 65 former staff members or students were serving in various capacities in government. The Training Division, under Leverett Lyon's direction, was proving to be the kind of practical school for public service which Mr. Brookings had envisioned. Between fifteen and twenty fellows were accepted annually for pre- or postdoctoral work in economics or government. Cooperative arrangements were worked out with Yale, Brown, Cornell, Radcliffe, Michigan, Virginia, Ohio State, Chicago, Kentucky, Pennsylvania, Wisconsin, and the Fletcher School of Law and Diplomacy to share the expenses of fellowships awarded to their advanced students, but fellows were accepted from many other institutions in this country and abroad. Among the 208 fellows in residence during the decade were Dana M. Barbour, Neil W. Chamberlain, Philip H. Coombs, Paul T. David, Edward F. Denison, James W. Fesler, A. D. H. Kaplan, James C. Nelson, Boris Shishkin, Harold M. Somers, Elmer B. Staats, Leroy D. Stinebower, and Kenneth O. Warner.

Brookings books were widely adopted as college texts and translated for the international scholarly community. Laurence Schmeckebier's *Government Publications and Their Use*, issued in 1936, provided a valuable reference work with its definitive codification and evaluation of the growing field of government publications. Arthur C. Millspaugh's studies of welfare organization and crime control focused on growing national problems. In 1938, Meriam issued his *Public Personnel Problems*, and the following year he and Schmeckebier summarized their views on government reorganization. Sumner Slichter's *Union Policies and Industrial Management*, in 1941, was recognized as a classic in the field of industrial jurisprudence. Schmeckebier's *Congressional Apportionment* developed the system of apportioning congressional representation among the states which was embodied in the Congressional Apportionment Act of 1941. Moulton, concerned with the need for wider dissemination of research findings, initiated a series of pamphlets summarizing the highlights of major studies.

In Europe, Hitler's war machine was on the march. In the spring of 1940, the Nazi blitzkrieg rolled through Holland, Belgium, and France, and Great Britain stood alone. As President Roosevelt moved a reluctant nation towards preparedness, the Institution moved to aid the administration with a series of studies of mobilization problems. Charles O. Hardy's *Wartime Control of Prices* was prepared at the request of the War Department and published more than a year before Pearl Harbor. When the United States went to war, it was the only comprehensive analysis of issues involved in price control and alternative methods of financing the war program which was then available to government agencies.

The trustees were notably active in the war effort. Board Chairman Dwight F. Davis took several members of the staff with him to England for a special study of British mobilization efforts. Shortly afterward, he was named Director General of the Army Specialist Corps. Others active in government service were Dean Acheson, Vannevar Bush, Karl T. Compton, and Edward R. Stettinius Jr.

As "Old Dr. New Deal" was replaced by "Dr. Win the War," Moulton laid aside his philosophic quarrel with the administration. President Roosevelt appointed him to the War Resources Board, responsible for studying the tentative mobilization plans of the defense agencies and making recommendations for improvements.

IV

WARTIME AND READJUSTMENT

Focus on Foreign Policy

Your report [Brookings' proposal for administering the Marshall Plan] is an amazingly fine and comprehensive piece of work . . . and you have come up with an answer and a recommendation which are (in my opinion) very sound. Just between us, I can say that with a very few alterations I could adopt the formula as my own. In any event, it is inevitable that your report will become the Congressional 'work-sheet' in respect to this complex and critical problem.

ARTHUR H. VANDENBERG TO HAROLD MOULTON
JANUARY 24, 1948

NINETEEN FORTY-ONE was a peak year for the Institution: new sources of foundation support had been attracted to the program, and operating revenues had reached $460,000. Now, as the nation went to war, financial support for research dried up and expansion plans were indefinitely postponed. Among the casualties of the emergency were projected institutes for mineral economics and economic research in aviation, a series of educational films, and a program of seminars by which Moulton had hoped to establish continuing relationships with Latin American scholars.

Once again, service projects became essential to survival. The staff was increasingly drawn into work for congressional committees drafting legislation to mobilize small business for war production, hammer out wartime labor policy, and provide emergency tax measures. Other studies conducted for government agencies examined the capacity of the steel and aluminum industries, wartime requirements for electric power, measures for control of automobile production, and needed changes in financial and statistical reporting for the Navy Department and the Budget Bureau.

By 1942, operating revenues were down to $312,000, the lowest in the history of the consolidated Institution. Nevertheless, its constructive work continued. A series of pamphlets examined the effects of the national defense program on the economy, the need for coordinated price policy, and methods of curtailing nondefense expenditures.

Harold Metz' *Is There Enough Manpower?*, published that fall, demonstrated that the government's plan for a 16 million-man armed force would seriously interfere with war production. Senator Bankhead of the Senate Appropriations Committee asked Metz to help him organize and analyze hearings, as a result of which the committee wrote a 12 million-man limitation into the armed forces appropriations.

Charles Dearing, whose *Automobile Transportation in the War Effort* was instrumental in setting policies for rationing of gas, tires, and automobile supplies, went to the Office of Defense Transportation to help determine military transport needs. Harold Rowe became Director of Food Rationing, later assistant director of food programs in the Foreign Economic Administration. Pasvolsky, back at the State Department as Hull's assistant, headed a task force on postwar planning.

Only a few members of the research staff remained. Millspaugh's massive study, *Democracy, Efficiency, Stability*, the forty-third in the series of studies in administration, became the last publication to bear the inscription of the Institute for Government Research: both Institutes were abolished as formal divisions and consolidated into a single research staff. The fellowship program was discontinued. From 1942 through 1947, the dormitories of the residence building were made available to internes of the National Institute of Public Affairs.

Nourse, who in 1942 served as president of the American Economic Association and chairman of the Social Science Research Council, was appointed Vice President of the Institution in 1943. In *Price Making in a Democracy*, 1944, he analyzed a broad area "between automatic and authoritarian price making" in which corporation executives have considerable discretionary power. The book argued that these executives' price-policies may be a major constructive force in the national economy, and recommended broad education of businessmen, with emphasis on the "public interest."

The staff provided consulting services to congressional committees and conducted studies of postwar demobilization and reconversion problems for Senator Walter George's Special Senate Committee on Post-War Economic Policy and Planning. Moulton continued his own research on the nature of the economic system, and planned a detailed postwar program for the Institution. He saw the need for placing increased emphasis on international developments and trends. He hoped to revitalize the fellowship program. Convinced that leaders in public and private life needed better opportunities to inform themselves on public issues, he blueprinted a conference program which would bring young executives in business and labor to Brookings for intervals of intensive discussion and study.

In the fall of 1945, Jerome Greene resigned from the board. "It is a great satisfaction to me as one of the group that founded the Institute for Government Research that thanks to the leadership of Mr. Brookings, the great generosity of Mr. and Mrs. Brookings and the wisdom and energy of your administration, The Brookings Institution has acquired a position of importance it holds today," he wrote Moulton. "I feel that it has every assurance of permanence now that its usefulness and public recognition are so thoroughly established."

But the permanence of the Institution was in some doubt. With the rest of the nation, it faced serious problems of postwar readjustment. The bomb on Hiroshima had sped the Japanese surrender but troubled the conscience of the world with the awesome potentialities of the atomic age. The federal government, with Harry Truman still new and uncertain in the White House, was faced with mounting problems at home and abroad. As 1946 began, arguments raged over the lifting of wartime controls. Tension was growing between business and labor. Prices were rising and consumer goods were scarce. In Europe, the growing threat of international communism was already evident.

Foundation support for Brookings had grown to sizable proportions by the end of the thirties, but during the war had dwindled as the number of research projects was reduced. Plans for expansion of research and restoration of the fellowship program were indefinitely postponed.

Moulton's investment policies provided a rising endowment income, which met half the Institution's reduced expenditures. Service projects again helped balance the budget. Pennsylvania requested a study of highway development; Iowa called for a taxation study. Memoranda on problems of government reorganization were prepared for the Senate Judiciary Committee and the House Committee on Expenditures of Executive Departments.

The Institution issued a series of pamphlets based on its work for the Special Senate Committee on Post-War Economic Policy and Planning. A study of the *Control of Germany and Japan*, by Moulton and Louis Marlio, found a ready market and was chosen by the Book-of-the-Month Club as a special selection for its 600,000 members. A volume by Lewis Kimmel analyzed post-war fiscal requirements at the federal, state, and local levels.

In 1946 Vice President Nourse, one of the original staff members of the Institute of Economics, resigned to accept appointment by President Truman as the first Chairman of the Council of Economic Advisers. For the next three years, he was to render distinguished service in the formulation of national economic policies and in focusing public attention on basic economic conditions and trends—work which tested the theories developed in his research at Brookings. Lewis Meriam, whose study of *Relief and Social Security* had just been issued, was named Vice President of the Institution.

Perkins Bass, former Governor of New Hampshire, brought new leadership to the trustees following the death of Dwight F. Davis. Among trustees joining the Board were William R. Biggs, Vice President of the Bank of New York; former Under Secretary of the Treasury Daniel W. Bell; and John J. McCloy.

As the nation slowly and reluctantly assumed its postwar role as a world power, the Institution developed a primary concern for international problems which was to characterize its work for the rest of the decade. In the spring of 1946, Leo Pasvolsky returned from the State Department, where he had held important posts throughout the war. He had served as executive director of the President's Advisory Committee on Postwar Foreign Policies, Secretary Hull's alternate in negotiations which established the International Monetary Fund and the International Bank for Reconstruction and Development, and head of the group drafting plans for a postwar international organization. At the San Francisco Conference, which brought the United Nations into being, he was deputy to Secretary Stettinius and chairman of the Coordination Committee that drafted the U.N. Charter. Later, he presided at the first meeting of the U.N. Preparatory Commission, served on the American delegation to the first meeting of the General Assembly, and was deputy U. S. representative on the Security Council.

Pasvolsky was acutely conscious of the growing need for research and education in international relations, both inside and outside the government. In an era in which foreign policy was destined to play a central role, he stated: "We can no longer afford, as in the past, to wait on events, to assume a largely passive attitude toward world affairs, to conduct our foreign relations on the basis of sporadic and often unrelated policies." Systematic research and education were needed to analyze this increasingly complex field, and an informed public opinion must be created for sound policy formulation.

Bringing with him a half-dozen experienced men and women who had served under him in the State Department, he established an International Studies Group and laid out an ambitious program of research and education. Financing was obtained from the Rockefeller Foundation, the Carnegie Corporation, and the Mellon Trust.

In 1947, Pasvolsky's International Studies Group issued the first of a series of annual surveys of *Major Problems of United States Foreign Policy*. To keep pace with rapid developments, these were supplemented by monthly reports on *Current Developments in United States Foreign Policy* and problem papers dealing in detail with specific issues such as the German peace settlement, the security of the Middle East, and Anglo-American economic relations. The materials were widely adopted for use in colleges and service academies.

In their publications, Pasvolsky and his staff used what he called the "problem approach" to provide a more realistic understanding of international policy issues and the decision-making process. The aim was to place the reader in the position of government officials faced with specific alternatives. The full range of domestic and international problems bearing on the issue was examined, and the feasible courses of action were analyzed to give the reader a basis for making his own policy recommendations.

Pasvolsky was concerned with the scarcity of trained specialists in international affairs—specialists who would be increasingly needed in government, business, and the growing number of public and private international agencies. The publications of the International

Studies Group were designed to provide background materials for a significant educational program aimed primarily at the academic community.

This ambitious educational program lasted for six years. By the time it concluded, over 1,000 scholars and top officials in government, the armed services, business, and labor had participated in national and regional seminars held across the country. They were subjected to intensive discussions of specific foreign policy issues such as European integration, economic assistance to Latin America, the veto in the United Nations, and the Soviet threat. Problem papers were provided in advance, and Brookings staff members helped focus the discussion on the consideration of alternatives for decision. Five national seminars, held at Hanover, New Hampshire; Stanford, California; Lake Forest, Illinois; and Denver, Colorado, drew participants from all the states for periods of one to two weeks. Seven regional seminars of three to five days' duration were held for educators and civic leaders within smaller geographic areas. All told, the series reached faculty members of 295 institutions.

In late 1947, the Institution was called upon to play a dramatic role in congressional passage of the historic European Recovery Program. Secretary of State George C. Marshall's bold and unprecedented plan to revive the shattered economy of Europe and to strengthen the Western nations against the communist threat had captured the imagination of the country, only to become mired in controversy over how it was to be administered. Widely differing proposals had been

Harold G. Moulton

1883–1965

advanced by the Harriman Committee, the State Department, and a congressional group headed by Christian Herter.

The Senate Foreign Relations Committee grappled with a seemingly insoluble problem: how to preserve the jurisdiction of the State Department over foreign policy, while providing for independent administration of the economic recovery program. On December 30, 1947, Chairman Arthur H. Vandenberg addressed a letter to Dr. Moulton requesting "a quick helping hand."

"From your own independent vantage—unrelated as you are to any of these rivalries—you are peculiarly well placed to give the Senate Foreign Relations Committee an independent recommendation," Vandenberg wrote. "Furthermore, the deep and universal respect which the Brookings Institution richly deserves and enjoys would make your recommendation of tremendous value to those of us who are struggling in the trenches with this conundrum. . . ."

Agreement on the administrative organization of ERP was essential to its success, as Vandenberg well knew. As soon as the Eightieth Congress began debate on the question in January 1948, the program ran into trouble from both the left and the right. Henry Wallace and his followers denounced the whole concept as a war-breeding, anti-Soviet "Martial Plan." On the other hand, Senator Robert Taft and his fellow conservatives were wary of the idea, complaining that it represented more "global New Dealism."

Pasvolsky assumed charge of the report and applied

his staff to completing the assignment, submitting it three weeks later. On January 24, Vandenberg released it with a statement endorsing its recommendations and citing the Institution's "voluntary labor in good citizenship and public service for which the Chairman of the Senate Committee on Foreign Relations wishes publicly to express his deep sense of appreciation."

In following weeks, Vandenberg worked quietly lining up the various factions behind the organizational principles outlined in the Brookings report. Some were persuaded by his willingness to compromise small details; others by mounting evidence of communist designs in Europe. On March 1, he rose in the Senate to plead for the legislation, noting "our great obligation to the Brookings Institution for the masterly job it did. The provisions in the pending bill largely follow its recommendations. I am happy to say the result already enjoys well-nigh universal approval in and out of Congress."

The European Recovery Program, he continued, "seeks peace and stability for free men in a free world. It seeks them by economic rather than by military means. . . . It recognizes the grim truth—whether we like it or not—that American self-interest, national economy, and national security are inseparably linked with these objectives."

It was a vivid moment in history. As Vandenberg finished his speech, dozens of Senators lined up to shake the hand of the long-time isolationist. All serious opposition had been undercut, and the bill passed the Senate and the House with large majorities. Four weeks later the Marshall Plan was law.

The Institution's work on economic and governmental problems was continuing, at a reduced level. A study of national labor policy by Harold Metz and Meyer Jacobstein in 1947 recommended reforms which were substantially embodied in the Taft-Hartley Law. In early 1948, the Hoover Commission on the Organization of the Executive Branch of the Government commissioned studies of transportation and public welfare. (Trustee Harold W. Dodds headed the Commission's Task Force on Personnel and Civil Service in the Federal Government.)

In a 1949 volume based on their report for the Hoover Commission, Charles L. Dearing and Wilfred Owen proposed a fundamental revision in national transportation policy. A study by Meriam and George W. Bachman for the Senate Committee on Labor and Public Welfare in 1948 called for improved data as a basis for national policy on health insurance, urging a systematic inventory of the nation's health facilities, which Bachman later provided in a massive study completed in 1952. In 1949, Moulton published his *Controlling Factors in Economic Development*, a synthesis of his theoretical work which stressed increasing productivity, expanding mass purchasing power, maintaining monetary and fiscal stability, and protecting natural resources as requirements for further dynamic development of the economy. In a 1950 study of *Cost and Financing of Social Security*, Meriam projected the need for a pay-as-you-go system that would use general revenues in addition to the trust funds.

But the International Studies Group provided the bulk of the Institution's research output, and attracted most of the foundation support. Operating revenues rose to almost $700,000 by 1949. The *Major Problems* series was now used in some 185 colleges and universities, and the third volume was selected by the American Political Science Association as the best publication of the year (1949) in the field of international relations.

Many proposals for changes in the United Nations were being widely debated, and Pasvolsky initiated a series of studies analyzing the principal issues. The International Studies Group was not without its critics, however. Its close ties with the State Department drew fire on the right with the arrival of the McCarthy era. The *Chicago Tribune* described the Institution in 1951 as "an odd mixture of conservatism and globaloney." In a feature article, the *Tribune* told its readers that "Brookings carries on an elaborate program of training and indoctrination in global thinking. Scholars are given 'problems' in foreign affairs that confront the United States and then form alternative policies. Most of the scholars wind up as policy makers in the State Department in Washington or in the Foreign Service abroad."

Curiously, the same activities were also attacked from the left. The fellow-traveling *New World Review*, reviewing the latest *Major Problems* volume in July 1952, charged that it did not present alternative solutions, but "merely different tactical approaches for achieving the aims of the billionaire American banks and trusts. . . . The reader is deluged with all the clichés and stereotypes which Secretary Acheson and John Foster Dulles have used to justify the policies they pursue. . . . The burden of the entire work is to justify the program for organizing war under the pretext of defending the 'free world' against 'Soviet aggression.' "

Vice President Meriam, one of the first senior staff members hired by Willoughby for the IGR in 1916, retired in 1951. To bring research results to broader public attention, Moulton established an Education Division headed by Charles A. H. Thomson, who had served as Staff Director of the President's Communications Policy Board in 1950. A report on the organization and administration of foreign affairs and overseas operations, prepared at the request of the Budget Bureau by a special staff under the direction of Paul David, made recommendations which paved the way for reorganization of the Economic Cooperation Administration and a broadening of the scope of its aid program.

Approaching the retirement age of 65, Moulton had submitted his resignation in 1948. For over a year the trustees searched for a successor, only to find that the best qualified men were not immediately available. At the Board's request, Moulton agreed to remain as President for three more years. In the spring of 1952 he brought his administration to a close, retiring at age 68.

Under his stewardship, the Institution's endowment had risen from $2.3 million to over $6.6 million, its annual budget from $365,000 to $858,000. The trustees, now headed by William R. Biggs as Chairman, recorded their "enduring sense of obligation and gratitude to Dr. Moulton for his long and distinguished service to the Institution as thoughtful scholar, prudent administrator, and imaginative leader."

THE MODERN ERA

A Broader Service

Today more than at any time in its history, the Brookings Institution is more nearly functioning as the men who founded it intended. . . . A salute is in order. Although Robert S. Brookings' interest in public affairs matured late in his life, nearly thirty years after his death his creative energy is affecting public administration and public policy more than ever.

PUBLIC ADMINISTRATION REVIEW, WINTER 1961

IN HIS LAST MONTHS before retirement, Moulton carefully avoided long-term commitments which might tie the hands of his successor. All work was fully financed, most projects were due to be completed within a year or two, and many of the staff were on short-term appointment. As a result, Robert D. Calkins assumed office as the second president of the Institution with wide latitude for action in charting its future course.

The new president faced fundamental problems, however. As *Business Week* put it in reporting the change in leadership, "talk about Brookings has concerned less what it was doing than what it had done." Except for the series of projects being conducted by the International Studies Group, there was no program of research: studies in progress reflected the random interests of the staff and the availability of foundation support for ad hoc projects. Some foundations now expressed reluctance to sponsor further studies because of the imbalance of the Institution's program—an imbalance created in large part by its long dependence on foundation policies of project financing.

As the "new boss for an old dream," Calkins recognized that drastic steps were necessary to build the kind of institution that Robert Brookings and Harold Moulton had envisioned. It was because he believed in the original dream that he had accepted the challenge.

An economist and administrator with broad experience in philanthropy and public affairs, Calkins brought special qualifications to the task of revitalizing the Institution. He had served since 1947 as Vice President and Director of the General Education Board. Previously he had been Dean of the School of Business at Columbia University and chairman of economics at the University of California, Berkeley, where he had built a first-rate department. As a mediator, arbitrator, and panel member of the War Labor Board, he had earned a reputation as a labor negotiator.

Calkins first set out to build a coherent research program. "Unless the Institution produces research that commands the respect of the scholarly community, it has nothing to offer the public," he told the trustees. All projects should be designed to provide "successive studies which will make a cumulative contribution in a chosen field of research." He appointed an advisory committee of leading social scientists to consider the appropriate functions, opportunities, and responsibilities of the Institution.

In the meantime, the decks had to be cleared. The operating budget was pruned drastically so that the Institution could operate within its own income until broader financing was available. As projects were completed the staff was reduced; unpromising projects were discontinued outright. The process of curtailment was sometimes painful: two grants totaling $192,000 were returned in full to the donor foundations to offset outstanding commitments for work being canceled, even though the funds had almost entirely been spent.

In the fall of 1952, funds ran out for the foreign policy conferences which had helped train a new generation of foreign policy specialists in colleges throughout the country. If the conferences were to be continued, it seemed appropriate that the academic institutions bear the responsibility. Subsequently the universities of Illinois, Michigan, Minnesota, and Wisconsin began a regional program as the Midwest Seminar on Foreign Policy, which continues to maintain an active program.

The sudden death of Leo Pasvolsky in the spring of 1953 forced a further re-evaluation of the activities of the International Studies Group. There was some sentiment for abandoning foreign policy studies altogether to concentrate on the Institution's historic interests in economics and government. Calkins argued for continuation: the United States had assumed a leadership role among the noncommunist nations, and with the Marshall Plan and Point Four Program had entered on long-term commitments to assist the economic and political development of countries throughout the free world. National problems in the future, he said, could be largely international: concentration on domestic issues could give the Institution a provincial outlook and seriously restrict the relevance of its work. The trustees gave their support, and by 1953 a research program had been outlined projecting continuing work in a variety of economic and governmental problem areas of both domestic and international policy.

The agonies of reappraisal were rewarded in 1954

with major grants for general support from both the Ford and Rockefeller foundations. Work began in earnest: a new professional staff was recruited, and initial studies commenced. By 1955, progress was sufficient to require the formal organization of three separate research divisions.

Calkins personally supervised the Economic Studies division, initiating studies in the fields of economic growth and stabilization, financial institutions and policies, government finance, competition and monopoly, and international economic problems. A. D. H. Kaplan's studies of competitive policies in big business, begun in the late 1940's, were issued in 1954. Wilfred Owen's *The Metropolitan Transportation Problem* broke new ground in 1956 by examining the relationships of transport development to urban living as a whole. *An Introduction to Economic Reasoning*, by Marshall A. Robinson, Herbert C. Morton, and James D. Calderwood, won wide acceptance as a text for schools, colleges, and adult discussion groups. At the request of the Council of Economic Advisers, the Institution served as host for a series of off-the-record conferences on the nation's economy which attracted leading specialists from government, business, and the universities.

Paul T. David was appointed to direct Governmental Studies. A Brookings Fellow in the early 1930's, he had served in the Budget Bureau and as a U. S. representative to the International Civil Aviation Organization before returning to the staff. With Ralph M. Goldman and Malcolm Moos, he conducted a major study of *Presidential Nominating Politics in 1952*, a project sponsored jointly by Brookings and the American Political Science Association. Their five-volume report, published in the spring of 1954, introduced new concepts of the relationship between presidential nominating patterns, leadership succession, and the United States political process. Building on this work, David initiated further studies of nominating and electoral processes.

Foreign Policy Studies were placed under the direction of Robert W. Hartley, who had come to Brookings from the State Department with Pasvolsky in 1946. Funds for the annual *Major Problems* volumes ran out, and the series had to be terminated. However, the United Nations studies Pasvolsky had projected were continued. The first two volumes, *The United Nations and the Maintenance of International Peace and Security*, by Leland M. Goodrich and Anne P. Simons, and *Proposals for Changes in the United Nations*, by Francis O. Wilcox and Carl M. Marcy, were issued in 1955. *The United Nations and Promotion of the General Welfare*, a comprehensive study by Robert E. Asher, Walter M. Kotschnig, William Adams Brown, Jr., James Frederick Green, Emil J. Sady, and associates, appeared two years later. Among other studies, the division prepared a 1956 report on administrative aspects of U. S. foreign assistance for the Senate's Special Committee to Study the Foreign Aid Program.

After the fellowship program ended in 1942, Brookings had little continuing contact with the broader world of scholarship, except through the regional seminars on foreign policy. Calkins obtained trustee approval to re-establish the fellowships with the Institution's funds, beginning in the fall of 1955. Graduate departments of leading institutions throughout the country were invited to nominate predoctoral or post-doctoral candidates working on policy problems in economics or government. To augment the staff for the developing research program, senior scholars from other institutions were appointed on a part-time or nonresident basis.

In the same year, President Calkins invited a small group of government executives and Brookings staff to explore the need for government training programs. They found that little was being done to improve the competence of top civil servants, in contrast to the opportunities open to senior officials in the military services and in business. Career officials typically rose through narrow channels in a single agency, and lacked any special training for broader responsibility. Many federal departments were, in fact, prohibited from spending public funds for such purposes.

Working closely with the Civil Service Commission and other government officials, the Brookings group planned a series of educational conferences which would combine concentrated reading and discussion of policy problems to give senior federal executives a broader understanding of government and their role in it. The Ford Foundation provided financing for this promising new means of strengthening the public service, and in 1957, Brookings began a two-year experiment to demonstrate its feasibility. William T. McDonald, executive vice chairman of the Civil Service Commission's Inter-Agency Advisory Group, was loaned to the Institution to direct the conferences. They were held in

Colonial Williamsburg, a historic setting which lent purpose to the discussions of leadership in democratic government.

"The purpose of the program," wrote Douglass Cater of *The Reporter*, "is not training but in the purest sense of the word, education. There is no desire to return the middle-aged career executive to a student-teacher relationship, which he is by temperament not prepared to accept. He is by definition a 'participant' in the conference, expected and encouraged to contribute as much of the dialogue as the visiting speakers. . . ." The objective was to stimulate ideas and an exchange of experience. Assisting in the process was a "faculty" selected from the nation's intellectual leadership: distinguished men and women from the universities, the Congress, the top echelons of the Executive branch, and the diplomatic and press corps.

"In concept, the Brookings Conference Program is truly revolutionary," Cater concluded. It recognized that the Civil Service had outgrown the physical dimensions of a "corps of clerks," and that the present-day career executive must "have a more thorough understanding of his role. He must be capable of comprehending the whole of government in order to comprehend better his part in it. . . ."

The Conferences for Federal Executives generated widespread interest in executive training activities throughout the government. The immediate and evident success of the program was a significant factor in the passage of the Government Employees Training Act of 1958, which for the first time made it possible for all federal agencies to release staff members for training at government expense. Participants returned to their agencies to establish similar programs for middle management executives. The Civil Service Commission began to develop the interdepartmental training programs which today offer hundreds of seminars and courses, many of them patterned on the Brookings model.

As the first results of the revitalized research program were being reviewed in scholarly journals, steps were taken to coordinate all publishing and dissemination activities. With the retirement of John K. Anderson, manager of publications since 1929, publication, production, and sales were merged with the editorial functions and the activities of the Education Division, which had issued a number of pamphlets based on Brookings research and produced three educational films circulated by Encyclopedia Britannica. The resulting Publications Division was placed under the direction of Herbert C. Morton, a former journalist and faculty member of Dartmouth's Amos Tuck School. Most Brookings books continued to be printed by the George Banta Company of Menasha, Wisconsin, which had prepared the Institution's publications since the early 1930's.

Then events threatened the momentum of the Institution's developing program. The Jackson Place headquarters, its home since 1931, was taken over by the government in early 1957 as the site for a future federal office building. Negotiations led to a three-year limit for vacating the premises.

Again, Brookings' President and trustees were forced

Robert D. Calkins

to make a fundamental decision. Temporary housing was considered; so were several suburban locations. Before action could be taken, a clear view of the Institution's future role was essential.

Out of this necessity, a larger vision emerged. Brookings would stay in downtown Washington, close to the vital center of public affairs and the primary sources of policy research. It would build a Center for Advanced Study three times larger than its old quarters, including extensive facilities for the scholarly community. Calkins asked the trustees to approve a plan which would finally realize the earlier dreams of Robert Brookings and Harold Moulton, and inaugurate a new era in the usefulness and relevance of the Institution's work:

"Too often we, as a people, have been intellectually unprepared for the problems of our times," his proposal declared. "By failing to anticipate and give thought to coming events, we have had to improvise for emergencies. . . . The means by which society marshals knowledge for the consideration of important domestic and international problems are seriously deficient. . . ."

The most important single step, he declared, was to build at least one national institution with the capacity to study emerging problems systematically. "It must be able to operate with imagination, distinction, and dispatch, unfettered by political controls or ties to special interests. It must offer a stimulating intellectual environment and provide challenging opportunities for important contributions to scholarship and public understanding. . . . The task of building the sort of institution needed is formidable, but it is imperative if we are to put knowledge more effectively to use."

The plan "nearly scared us to death," one of the trustees later admitted. It called for capital funds totaling $9 million to construct the Center, an annex for other nonprofit and educational organizations, and a conference center. To strengthen the staff and further expand the research and education program, it called for endowment and operating funds sufficient to double the annual operating budget, then at the level of $1 million a year. The concept was approved "subject to financing." A suitable site was located on Massachusetts Avenue, just east of Dupont Circle, and over the next year the land was assembled.

The plan was laid before Ford Foundation President Henry Heald and his associates. They acted with dispatch, endorsing the concept of a larger role for Brookings. In the fall of 1958, the Foundation made a grant of $5 million for ten-year support of the Institution's developing program, and $1.2 million toward construction of the Center for Advanced Study. The latter grant was matched by other foundations and private individuals, and construction began in early 1959. The Rockefeller Foundation gave $500,000 toward the cost of another building to house other related nonprofit organizations.

By the fall of 1960, when the Center was formally dedicated, the plans which had seemed so ambitious three years earlier were already largely realized. The Institution's research was winning increasing respect and attracting able scholars from universities and the government: the professional staff had grown from 34 in 1954 to 60, augmented by researchers from other institutions associated on various studies. Annual operating expenditures, which had totaled $650,000 in 1954, were approaching $2 million.

Ralph J. Watkins, former head of research for Dun & Bradstreet Inc., was named Director of the Economic Studies division in late 1957. Marshall A. Robinson's *The National Debt Ceiling* provided a timely appraisal which was useful in congressional debate on the issue in 1959. The following year John G. Gurley and Edward S. Shaw, in *Money in a Theory of Finance*, broadened the scope of traditional monetary analysis and formulated a theoretical basis for reassessment of existing concepts. Technical assistance missions were sent to Korea and South Vietnam to work on taxation and budget reforms.

A long-range national program of research in taxation and public expenditures, Studies of Government Finance, was established in 1960 with the support of the Ford Foundation. Joseph A. Pechman of the Committee for Economic Development, a tax economist who had served with the Council of Economic Advisers staff and the Treasury Department, was selected as Executive Director. The Brookings Trustees appointed a national committee to supervise the program. A series of studies and educational activities were planned to involve economists throughout the country in an unprecedented examination of public finance issues at the federal, state, and local levels.

In 1958, George A. Graham succeeded Paul David as

director of the Governmental Studies division. A professor of politics and former chairman of the department at Princeton University, he had served in government with the Budget Bureau and the Hoover Commission. Marver H. Bernstein's *The Job of the Federal Executive*, issued in that year, began a notable series of studies examining needs for strengthening the public service and improving departmental leadership and management.

By 1960, the division's earlier work reached fruition in a landmark series of studies of nominating and electoral processes. *The Politics of National Party Conventions*, by Paul David, Ralph Goldman, and Richard C. Bain, provided an authoritative study of presidential nominations and national party conventions. A companion volume summarized historical data on nominating conventions. Others examined the role of television in elections and analyzed the problems of creating an informed electorate.

Presidential Transitions, by Laurin Henry, focused attention on the critical process of transition between national administrations. His work served as background for an unprecedented series of papers prepared by the Brookings staff for the Republican and Democratic presidential candidates, summarizing major problems and issues to be faced by an incoming administration and suggesting alternative ways of dealing with them. In his memoir, *Kennedy*, Theodore Sorensen later described how these memoranda served as an agenda for President-elect John F. Kennedy and his top lieutenants on the morning after the election. Brookings, he wrote, "deserves a large share of the credit for history's smoothest transfer of power between opposing parties. . . ."

In the Foreign Policy Studies division, the bulk of Pasvolsky's program was completed. Ruth B. Russell's definitive *History of the United Nations Charter* was issued in 1958. The following year the division made a study of the formulation and administration of U. S. foreign policy for the Senate Foreign Relations Committee. The report, by H. Field Haviland and associates, made major recommendations for organization of the policy-making process. Haviland, a former Haverford College professor who joined the staff in 1956, was named Director in 1960 to succeed Robert Hartley, who had assumed chief responsibility for the Institution's building plans as Vice President for Administration in 1957.

Meanwhile the innovations of the Federal Executive Conferences had developed into a substantial educational program. Two years of experimentation had demonstrated that government agencies would cooperate in releasing participants for one- and two-week educational conferences, and that busy executives would take time out from their duties to exchange views with colleagues and informed specialists. Several agencies asked that the conferences be continued on a fee basis for their executive personnel. It was apparent that similar programs could be designed to meet the needs of executives in private life.

To conduct these activities, a separate operating division was established in 1959. James M. Mitchell,

Associate Director of the National Science Foundation, was appointed to direct them. First known as the Conference Program on Public Affairs, the division was designated the Advanced Study Program in 1962.

A former Civil Service Commissioner and Deputy Assistant Secretary of Defense for Manpower and Personnel, Mitchell was also one of the founders of the conference program, having served on the study group that planned the initial proposal. He and Calkins saw the division as a new kind of institution of higher education, providing special opportunities for leaders in all walks of life to keep abreast of research findings in the social sciences and to deepen their understanding of complex policy issues. The Advanced Study Program brought an added dimension to Brookings' historic objective of bringing knowledge to bear on public problems: its activities would not only disseminate relevant research to responsible persons in public and private life; they would help make the research itself more relevant by testing its findings and recommendations against the practical experience of operating officials.

Appointments to the Board of Trustees continued to reflect the Institution's close relations with government: former Assistant Secretary of State George McGhee; William C. Foster, former Administrator of the Economic Cooperation Administration; former Governor of Virginia Colgate W. Darden, Jr.; former Secretary of Health, Education, and Welfare Marion B. Folsom. In 1961, William Biggs relinquished the chairmanship of the Board which he had led through twelve years of transition and remarkable growth to become chairman of the executive and finance committees. Morehead Patterson, Chairman of the Board of American Machine and Foundry Company and former U. S. delegate to the U. N. Disarmament Commission, was elected Chairman.

The advent of the Kennedy Administration in 1961 gave the nation a new awareness of the uses of research and the contributions of scholarship to decision-making. Brookings was called on with increasing frequency. A report on *Proposed Studies on the Implications of Peaceful Space Activities for Human Affairs* suggested a research agenda for the National Aeronautics and Space Administration. Staff members served on several of the task forces which enlisted the intellectual community in planning New Frontier policies and programs. James Mitchell headed a Task Force on Training and Orientation for the Agency for International Development, while Roy Crawley directed a committee responsible for planning the recruitment of executive talent for the new agency. Wilfred Owen headed a policy-planning group established by the Secretary of Commerce to review transportation policy; Richard Goode served on the President's Commission on the Status of Women; Walter S. Salant was deputy leader of a State Department economic survey team in Indonesia. George Graham was appointed to the Budget Bureau's Advisory Committee on Productivity Measurement. Joseph Pechman served on the task force on economic policy and on the Consultants panel of the Secretary of the Treasury.

As the Institution's program expanded, President Calkins moved to broaden its base of support. In May

1962, he proposed a five-year, $20 million drive to finance further diversification of staff, intensification of research on public problems, and enlargement of educational activities for leaders in public and private life. His choice of a five-year period was deliberate. With his own retirement scheduled for 1968, he intended to ensure an orderly transition and long-term financial stability for the Institution. A search was begun for a Vice President for Program who could succeed him.

The trustees supported the development plans, although some were doubtful that the funds could be obtained in the period projected. To make further sources available, they authorized solicitation of general support from business firms in the fall of 1962, recognizing a national trend toward unrestricted corporate giving for education and other public purposes.

Morehead Patterson, who had strongly backed Calkins' plans, died suddenly in August 1962. Under his successor as Chairman, Eugene R. Black, former President of the International Bank for Reconstruction and Development, the plans were carried forward.

The Institution's list of economic studies was growing. In 1961, Walter Salant and Beatrice N. Vaccara, in *Import Liberalization and Employment*, made the first detailed analysis of the effect of tariff reduction and removal of import barriers on domestic employment. Among other volumes issued were J. M. Clark's theoretical study of *Competition as a Dynamic Process* and Herman M. and Anne R. Somers' timely *Doctors, Patients, and Health Insurance*. In 1962 came John P. Lewis' perceptive study of India's development problems, *Quiet Crisis in India*; Mark Massel's examination of legal and economic issues in *Competition and Monopoly*; Joseph W. Garbarino's *Wage Policy and Long-Term Contracts*; and James A. Maxwell's penetrating study of *Tax Credits and Intergovernmental Fiscal Relations.*

With the retirement of Ralph Watkins that summer, Joseph Pechman was appointed Director of Economic Studies. Pechman's Studies of Government Finance program was exerting marked influence in the field. Some of the nation's leading economists undertook projects and put their graduate students to work on others, while top officials of the Treasury and the Budget Bureau were regular participants in the research conferences.

Among early Studies of Government Finance volumes were Wilfred Lewis, Jr.'s *Federal Fiscal Policy in the Postwar Recessions* assessing its impact on the economy and implications for the future; Richard Goode's definitive study of *The Individual Income Tax*; and a series summarizing the findings of experts' conferences held to narrow the range of disagreement on controversial issues such as oil depletion allowances, taxation of state and local securities, measuring benefits of government investments, and tax treatment of foreign income. Other studies provided nontechnical guides for the layman on complex issues of budget and tax policy and state and local finance. By the time the program concludes its work in 1967, it will have produced over twenty-five volumes, hundreds of articles, and some fifty doctoral dissertations.

A major program of transportation research was

initiated by the division in 1962 under a five-year grant from the Agency for International Development. A team of transport economists was assembled under Wilfred Owen, and studies were designed to advance the state of knowledge about the role of transportation in economic development with the cooperation of scholars from other institutions. Some two dozen studies and reports will be completed by 1967.

Nineteen sixty-three brought further expansion of economic research. Several years earlier a group of scholars had constructed an econometric model of the U. S. economy for the Social Science Research Council; Brookings was now asked to assume responsibility for the model and for overseeing its continued revision and improvement. With support from the National Science Foundation the Institution took over the work, recruiting an interuniversity team of econometricians. Useful for short-term forecasting and for analysis of the determinants of growth, price level changes, balance-of-payments positions, income distribution, and other basic questions, the model will make Brookings a national center for study of the structural properties of the economy.

One of the Institution's major contributions to public-policy discussions in the last decade was its 1963 study of the U. S. balance of payments outlook, directed by Walter Salant. Prepared as a report to the Council of Economic Advisers, it demonstrated the Institution's capacity to illuminate an important and difficult issue. Salant's analysis went beyond conventional thinking and pointed the way to new solutions for the problems created by a shortage of international liquidity.

The government decided not to issue the report itself because of hesitation over several aspects of the controversial recommendations, and Brookings promptly moved to publish it. The manuscript was completed by the time the Joint Economic Committee of Congress opened its hearings on the balance of payments problem, and the committee was permitted to release a special edition of the report for prompt consideration of its findings prior to publication.

Described by the committee as "a major document for policy-makers and the public," the report became the focal point for the hearings. Within two years, its recommendation for increasing international liquidity had become accepted as a basic principle of international monetary policy.

By the mid-1960's, economic studies were being published at the rate of twenty a year, and some sixty projects were in progress in the fields of growth and stability, fiscal and tax policies and institutions, international trade, technological change, and human resources.

Governmental Studies research in the 1960's drew attention to serious policy considerations involved in the federal impact on college and university teaching, research and administration. Harold Orlans' *Effects of Federal Programs on Higher Education* served as a focus of several congressional inquiries. Prepared for the U. S. Office of Education, it helped direct attention to the heavy concentration of government funds in a few universities and fields, and its resultant adverse effects in undergraduate education and liberal arts colleges. (After the Office of Education published a summary omitting certain criticisms of federal research policies, Brookings invoked the clause in all its government contracts protecting the right to publish its findings, and issued the entire report.) Charles L. Clapp's *The Congressman: His Work as He Sees It*, based on a series of seminars for congressmen, also attracted wide attention for its authoritative account.

The findings of a 1963 study of *Professional Personnel for the City of New York* by David T. Stanley, were promptly endorsed and partially implemented by the city administration. In 1964, government policies for the recruitment, retention, and development of personnel were significantly affected by the findings of *The Image of the Federal Service*, by Franklin P. Kilpatrick, Milton C. Cummings, Jr., and M. Kent Jennings. A pioneering study of how government employment is viewed by various segments of the population, it amassed data which will provide useful bench marks for future comparative research. These and later Brookings studies were cited by the Public Personnel Association in 1964 as exerting an influence "far beyond the national government. The findings and techniques . . . in many cases apply equally to personnel considerations in state and local government in this country and around the world."

Laurin Henry's studies of the transition between national administrations produced legislative results. He had recommended that the heavy expenses borne by incoming administrations before taking office be covered by regular appropriations "since it is clearly in the public interest to have the next administration ready to operate as completely as possible on inauguration day." As a consultant to the Budget Bureau, he helped draft a bill to accomplish this. The measure was passed by Congress and signed into law by President Johnson in 1964.

A continuing group of scholars, public officials, and others concerned with the improvement of the public service, meeting under the auspices of the division since 1958, has played a significant role in the development of its research on problems of the Executive branch. The Conference on the Public Service has also played a broader role in stimulating discussion of federal personnel and management issues. Members of Congress and key legislative and executive staff members have been closely involved in studies of party policy and organizational issues in both Houses through participation in a series of seminars related to individual projects.

A Ford Foundation grant in 1965 inaugurated a major staff investigation of problems involved in the administration of estates in bankruptcy. Studies are also under way on the selection and performance of federal judges, as part of a developing program of research on the administration of justice.

The Foreign Policy Studies division in the early 1960's outlined a five-year program of research on the political, economic, and social development of the emerging nations. A group of specialists were brought together to explore the sensitive field of political development, and their discussions helped bring about a searching reappraisal of policies within the State Department. Another conference developed an agenda for research to improve the effectiveness of assistance to the developing countries. Foreign assistance remained a central concern: Robert Asher's *Grants, Loans, and Local Currencies* in 1961 examined the relative benefits of the various forms of aid, and later studies analyzed the results of unilateral and multilateral aid operations. Other important areas were treated in studies of disarmament, the role of the United States in Southeast Asia, and the role of labor unions in developing countries.

The primary emphasis of new research, however, was on Latin America. In cooperation with nine Latin American research institutions, a program was established which will provide basic data for spurring the economic progress of the region and strengthening the efforts of the Latin American Free Trade Association toward economic integration. Other studies of political and social development in selected Latin American countries were begun to lay the groundwork for needed readjustments in U. S. policies toward the emerging countries of the world.

Continuing interest in the problems of international organization led to another program of studies evaluating the work of the United Nations and the specialized agencies in such fields as peacekeeping, development assistance, and human rights. Designed in close consultation with the Department of State, the program focuses on major problems of interest to the U. S. government.

In 1966, Brookings took steps to apply the quantitative and computational methods of advanced electronic data processing to its research. A Computer Center was established to aid work in each of the research divisions. It will also undertake general investigations into the relationships between computer science and the social sciences.

The Advanced Study Program has provided an increasing variety of opportunities to communicate research knowledge to leaders in public and private life. Under Walter G. Held, a public administration specialist and former U. S. Chamber of Commerce aide, conferences for businessmen have been expanded. Each year, some 200 executives participate in special programs designed to improve their understanding of government activities, problems, and policy issues. A similar series is held for top elective officers of national and international labor unions. A Public Affairs Fellowship Program brings businessmen to Washington for five months of seminars at Brookings and work in policy-making offices of federal agencies.

Under Fordyce Luikart and Harry R. Seymour, former senior government officials, the Williamsburg conferences for federal executives have been extended to include all of the departments and independent agencies. Programs have been designed for scientists and science administrators, general counsels, investigative officers, budget officers, and other specialists as well as general administrators. Special conferences for congressmen, senators, and their staffs have brought significant research developments to their attention. Federal Executive Fellowships permit senior career civil servants to study at Brookings on leave from their agencies. Groups of federal officials have been brought together with top business leaders to gain a better insight into the operations and problems of major corporations. New conferences have been initiated for officials of state governments. Civic leaders and urban officials in major metropolitan areas have been brought together for regional Urban Policy Conferences led by John Osman, former vice president of the Fund for Adult Education, in a series designed to apply relevant social science research to their local problems.

"The impact of this trail-blazing education program has been tremendous," the Public Personnel Association declared in presenting its 1964 Award for Merit to Brookings. "It directed attention to needed training for top-level career officials, heretofore neglected. It demonstrated the value of innovations. It provided leadership that stimulated executive development programs in many federal departments. And finally, it created a model for similar efforts in state and local governments." By 1966, some 3,300 senior civil servants and high-ranking military officers and 3,200 top officials from the business community, labor, Congress, and state and local government had participated in Advanced Study Program activities.

Through the Brookings Research Fellowships, the Institution has made a growing contribution to the development of younger scholars engaged in policy research. Since they were re-established in 1955, seventy-seven have been awarded. Service to the broader intellectual community has been extended in other ways: each year more than fifty visiting scholars from institutions throughout the country and abroad come to the

Institution to carry out their own research, and hundreds of others in the Washington area regularly use its dining and conference facilities. Opening of the east building in 1963 provided a home for two dozen other nonprofit research and educational organizations.

As the products of the research divisions have increased from a handful of books to a current rate of twenty-five books a year, the Publications Division enlarged its efforts to disseminate findings. Since 1962, eight-page Research Reports have been issued concurrently with each study to highlight its findings. Articles by staff in scholarly publications are issued in a Reprint Series. Arrangements have been made with commercial publishers to reprint paperback editions of Brookings studies. A quarterly *Bulletin* provides some 20,000 readers with a brief description of new developments in the Institution's program. Detailed annual reports have been published since 1961.

In the spring of 1965, Budget Director Kermit Gordon came to Brookings as Vice President and heir apparent. A Rhodes Scholar, Gordon had taught at Williams College for fifteen years and had directed the Ford Foundation's economic development activities for a year before coming to Washington in 1961 as a member of the Council of Economic Advisers. Calkins had sought to interest him in the post in 1963 and 1964, but he was deeply committed to his Budget role under Presidents Kennedy and Johnson, both of whom gave unprecedented weight to economic analysis in formulating public-policy decisions. Now, after four years at the top echelons of federal policy-making, he was ready to help lead Brookings toward further research contributions in the public interest.

Given full responsibility for the research and educational program, Gordon began planning more quick-impact studies of current policy issues, and a series of cost-benefit studies of federal activities. "Numerous steps have been taken in recent years to elevate the quality of program evaluation in the federal government, but independent research can play a vital role in speeding this trend," he explained. "Sharper tools of analysis can raise standards of program evaluation and bring about wiser use of resources, sounder planning and management of federal programs, and substantial benefits for the private economy. The opportunities for useful research in this field are enormous."

With vigorous future leadership of the Institution assured, Calkins sought to give it a sound financial basis before the end of his administration. The budget was now well over $3 million. A growing number of foundations were supporting the work of the Institution. More than sixty corporations had become annual contributors. Under William Biggs' investment management, endowment had risen to $12 million. Income on these investments, however, provided only about one-seventh of the operating budget. Except for the gifts of Mr. and Mrs. Brookings, few capital grants had been received by the Institution since its founding. The research program was still heavily dependent on project financing, with its attendant limitations.

The extraordinary development of the Institution was made possible by the general support grants of the

Ford and Rockefeller Foundations in the 1950's, but these funds were now tapering off. Ironically, as Brookings entered the most productive period in its history, drastic reductions in staff and program would be required unless major new financing could be found.

Again Calkins laid a major proposal before President Henry Heald of the Ford Foundation. New capital funds and long-term support were essential, he stressed, if Brookings was to make effective use of its unique capabilities and advantages for policy research and the education of decision-makers:

Brookings is in a position to make constructive contributions in many areas where government agencies are restricted by their own interests, by political considerations, or by the controversial nature of the problem. . . .

One of the principal obstacles to policy research [in the academic community] is the difficulty of mobilizing the manpower and range of skills necessary to examine a complex subject in depth. . . . Brookings builds such interdisciplinary competence into its own staff. . . . When additional specialists are needed, the Institution can draw upon the talents of the intellectual community at large by assembling temporary staff. . . .

As a nonpartisan center in Washington where scholars and responsible leaders in government and private life gather daily, Brookings provides unequalled opportunities for scholars to test their ideas against the realities of day-to-day operations, and for decision-makers in and out of government to deepen their awareness of new social science knowledge and its relevance for policy.

In December 1965, the Ford Foundation responded with a grant of $14 million, the largest ever received by the Institution. Ten million of it was to be used as capital endowment, the balance for general support over the next decade.

"For the past half-century, Brookings has occupied a special place on the Washington scene," Henry Heald noted. Because of its close ties to both the academic community and the world of affairs, he said, the Institution was "uniquely fitted to play a central role" in the growing effort to place knowledge at the service of mankind.

For the first time in its history, the Institution was assured that it could maintain independently and indefinitely a substantial operating program in the public interest. Calkins sent word of the grant to Harold Moulton, then seriously ill. Days before his death on December 14, the first president of the Institution, who had guided it through its most critical period, expressed his pleasure with the news.

Additional assurance that the future of the Institution was secure was provided by Mrs. Robert Brookings, who had supported and watched its development with loyal interest for forty years until her death on April 7, 1965. Shortly before receipt of the Ford grant, the Institution was notified of a bequest from her estate equivalent to some $8 million.

With these major grants, the Institution had already surpassed the $20 million capital development goal President Calkins had hoped to reach by 1968. There would be further needs, he cautioned: "In government and in the private sector the formulation of sound policies to deal with the problems of our times will require ever more penetrating examination of goals and alternatives; more systematic appraisal of existing policies and institutions; and more attention to equipping leaders to deal with a changing world."

In each of these areas, he could add with certainty, Brookings would be able to make a greater contribution in its second half-century. But in the future, as in the first fifty years, the Institution's effectiveness would ultimately depend on men and women with faith in the value of knowledge as a guide to public policy.

THE BROOKINGS INSTITUTION

722 Jackson Place, N.W., Washington, D.C.

1932–1960

Index

THIS BOOK WAS SET IN MONOTYPE JANSON

PRINTED ON CURTIS RAG PAPER AND BOUND

BY THE GEORGE BANTA COMPANY

MENASHA, WISCONSIN

DESIGNED BY ROLAND A. HOOVER